THE PROFOUND PHILOSOPHICAL PONTIFICATIONS OF BIG JOHN DEACON

Freemason Extraordinaire

Volume II

JAMES "CHRIS" WILLIAMS IV

Perfect Ashlar Publishing

Universal City, TX

For ordering information please visit Perfect Ashlar Publishing's website at:
www.PerfectAshlarPublishing.com

ISBN: 978-1-7362557-4-2 (Print)

Cover art by Meforya (Mehanaaz H.) For permission requests, email to the artist directly at the email address mehnaazhusain@gmail.com.

DEDICATION

To my Brothers of Davy Crockett Lodge, who supported and encouraged me to keep writing, especially, Brother Brad Kohanke and his wife, Crystal and Brother Burt Reynolds and his wife Ana, who compiled the first two years of my stories and presented them to me in book form, which showed me that this book series was possible.

To William A. Smith for assisting my Brothers in that early project.

This book is dedicated to my family: JC, Tiffany, Brenda, Aaron, Sarah, Kelli, Megan, Travis, Chandler, and Jordan; along with all my other unofficial proofreaders. I cannot express enough how important you all were.

To all my Masonic Brothers who do what Masons do, have provided the story lines and situations in the John Deacon series. Thank you all for being my Brothers! I hope somehow Brother John has both entertained and educated you. If so, I have accomplished my purpose.

To my Dad, James C. Williams III, the ultimate and authentic cowboy, and my Mom Billye, thank you both for a lifetime of ideas and inspiration.

And finally, to my wife Pam, who makes my life what it is. Without her support, none of this could have happened.

TABLE OF CONTENTS

FOREWORD

Throughout my masonic career, I have, of course, learned countless valuable lessons; many of those lessons came from Brother John Deacon. I was introduced to brother John in March of 2009 by one of my great mentors, Brother Chris Williams. Chris and I became the closest of friends during that time, he was the Worshipful Master of Davy Crockett Lodge, and I served as his Senior Warden. When Chris began regaling his Brethren with stories of this larger-than-life customer who wandered into his shop one spring day, we all listened in awe. I'm not sure if we realized at that time that while these often-hilarious exploits were entertaining us, we were also learning invaluable lessons about freemasonry.

John Deacon is a Texas Mason, through and through. From his large stature to his Stetson Silverbelly hat to his long Texas drawl, we could pick him out of a crowd anywhere. We all know someone in our lodge who reminds us of John. He is that past master who always has a sage piece of advice. John might not make it to lodge for every stated meeting or degree, but when he does, everyone in the room is glad to see him (and can't miss him). When he isn't with his Brethren, he is thinking about them and anxious for a time when he can sit in the lodge with them again. John is the past master who seems to take everyone under his wing; after all, he has had quite a masonic career and has a lot to offer the masonic fraternity. For John Deacon, there is never a time when there are no designs upon the trestle board; he understands that there is much work still to be done for the good of the order.

In this second volume of The Profound Philosophical Pontifications of Big John Deacon, we again catch up with brothers John Deacon and

Chris Williams and join them for more hilariously educational tales of what it means to be a good friend and Brother. The pair reminds us those good Masons are proud of their craft and spread the cement that unites us all. By their lessons, we are reminded that we aren't made into Masons simply by going through a few rituals; it takes years of work, learning, and sharing to become what our rituals teach us we should be. These stories help us understand that, while Masonry would take every good man by the hand, it is incumbent upon us Masons to continue educating those good men by diffusing that Great Light.

Now, as we rejoin Chris and John, let us open our hearts and minds so that their stories may continue to encourage us along our Masonic journey. May their words help us to see things in a new light that gives us that renewed spirit our craft so desperately needs. And finally, may Brotherly love prevail and every moral and social virtue cement us.

-Amen

William Burt Reynolds,

Past Master, Davy Crockett Lodge No. 1225

San Antonio, Texas

HOGS, GOATS, AND RODEO FOOD

I have to tell you that he has a knack for interrupting me at the most inopportune times. Who the heck am I talking about? I am talking about Brother John Deacon, that's who. Pam went shopping with her friend, and since I was alone with about four hours to kill, I thought I would sneak in a little nap. Just as my head hit the pillow, the phone rang. I thought about not looking at the caller ID, and then when I did, I considered not answering it, but I did not want to regret it later. I answered and immediately regretted my decision.

At first, I was a little confused because I heard grunting noises in the background. I am sure you can imagine without telling you what I thought was going on. I almost hung up right then.

"*Brother Chris!*" Brother John shouted, while huffing and puffing into the phone. "*Hold on a second!*"

"*John, what are you doing!*" I yelled back. As I listened, it sounded like he was in some kind of a scuffle or something. Just as I was about to hang up, he came back on and abruptly asked, "What are you doing right now?"

"Well, I was going to take a nap, but after what I heard the last thirty seconds, I don't think I could sleep if I wanted to."

"Oh, cut it out," he growled. "Why don't you come down here and help me."

"Are you kidding? I am not driving five hours to see you on a Saturday afternoon."

"I'm not asking you to, I am down here at the Stock Show and Rodeo. I need your help."

I was instantly confused, which is nothing new. I knew our Rodeo was going on, but John lived a long way from here. "You mean our Rodeo?"

That got him to sputtering and spitting like he swallowed something the wrong way, "Gol-durn-it Brother Chris, you are wasting my time here. I am hanging on to a huge ol' hog that's dang near as big as I am. I need your help." I have to tell you that many pictures ran through my mind on my way down to the Rodeo Grounds, and none were pleasant.

When I got there, it took me a while to locate John. He was in the swine barn, and to my surprise, he was actually in the middle of the show ring judging hogs. He never ceases to amaze me. When John saw me, he waved me down to the gate where I met him. He told me that he was glad I was there and needed help with a problem child. "Follow me."

As we walked, John told me that he was a swine judge at stock shows and had been doing that for many years. From time to time he also showed some of his hogs. I followed him to another barn that was back in a far corner. John stopped in front of a trailer that had been backed into the door. Inside was the biggest hog I think I have ever seen. This giant hog looked up at me and gave a little grunt and then just mean mugged John.

"I don't think he likes you much, John."

"No kidding," John replied sarcastically. "I have been trying to get this here pain in the rear hog out of this trailer into a pen for the last two hours. I have used up all my favors with the boys here, and now they won't help me. This hog is just mean. I know you spent time around livestock on the ranch, and you are my last hope."

"John, I am confused. This is a show barn. This is where they show livestock. This hog doesn't look like he wants to be shown."

"Oh, he's ok, Brother Chris. He just gets an attitude every once in a while. Once I get him out of this trailer and into a pen, he'll be alright."

"Yeah, right," I said skeptically. "He looks like he has more than an attitude." I had never done much with hogs, mostly just horses and cattle. I really wasn't looking forward to this, but I helped John fix up a makeshift chute that would head the hog into that pen once we, or rather if, we got him out of the trailer. Before we entered the trailer, I suggested to John that we just use a come-a-long and pull him out approach. That got me a nasty look. I decided to call Pam and tell her I loved her before following John into that trailer.

I knew that one of the ways you guide a hog was to grab his tail and kind of steer him the way you want him to go, so I decided I was going to handle the hind end of him. John eased up to the big guy, who started to grunt louder and faster the closer John got. John approached him like a Sumo Wrestler ready to clinch. What happened next, no one could have predicted.

Dear Reader,

I want you to know that a six hundred and fifty-pound hog can move pretty quick when he wants to.

Well, just as John was reaching down to try to get him to stand up, he shot to his feet and headed for the trailer gate at a high rate of speed, grunting and squealing as he went. John dove and grabbed him around the neck like a Steer Wrestler, and I dang near missed grabbing his tail on the way by. That crazy hog shot out the back of that trailer at a full sprint squealing louder than ever with John hanging on for dear life. As for me, well, let's just say it was hard to steer him while I was bouncing off the sides of the fencing on either side of the chute. It took every ounce of strength for me just to hang on. Everything was a blur, and I could hear yelling and even some cheering. We were dragged, yes dragged, across that barn by that devil's spawn excuse for a hog. In the moment, I was mad as Hell. In a split second I made up my mind that when we stopped, I would make ham and eggs out of this hog; then I was going to deal with Brother John for bringing me down here in the first place. The whole ordeal ended when I bounced off a fence post as the hog passed through the gate into his pen. It seemed like twenty minutes had passed, but it couldn't have been more than forty-five seconds at the most as fast as porky was running.

I laid there for a few seconds catching my breath, and when I looked up, I saw that unholy pork monster laying down as calm and as peaceful as anything. John had released his death grip from that hog's neck and rolled over on his back, breathing hard to my left. I pushed myself up to my knees and realized that both my arms were scratched and rubbed raw from that seventy-five-yard dragging across the swine barn. The front of my pants was filled up with a mixture of dirt, hay, and pig manure. All the buttons on my shirt had been rubbed off. If that wasn't enough, I had lost one shoe and my hat somewhere along the way. As I finally got to my feet, my attention was drawn back to the noise around us. When I looked, I saw a bunch of people gathered around the pen. Some were clapping, and some were hootin and hollerin, but most were just downright laughing at us.

I shook my head and cleared some of the cobwebs out just as John stood up. He looked around with a sheepish grin on his face and turned to me. He started to say something just as my anger surfaced again, I charged that mean mound of pork with the full intent of doing major damage. I really don't know what I thought I would do to that huge blob of blubber, but I was so mad I was going to do something. I launched myself at him as John tried to catch me. I landed hard on top of that hog and started punching and kicking as hard as I could. After a few seconds, I looked up to see the hog just calmly looking at me. I was totally out of breath. I just laid there on top of him, sucking in big gulps of air. Finally, John came over, picked me up, carried me out of the pen, and closed the gate.

People were still talking about our warp-speed trip from trailer to pen. One old-timer stopped laughing long enough to ask us if we could get his hogs out of his trailer. He stepped back quickly when he saw the look in my eyes. John reached out and grabbed me.

"Come on, Brother Chris. Let's go clean up a bit."

I was completely unprepared for the person that was looking back at me from the mirror. There was no doubt I was going to be plenty sore tomorrow. We washed up as much as we could, and John offered to buy me some good old Rodeo food. Right outside the swine barn was a Texas BBQ stand where he bought four BBQ beef sandwiches and half a rack of pork ribs. I thought we were going to sit and eat, but I was wrong. He grabbed his food and walked (with everyone we passed staring at us) over to a little stand selling roasted corn on the cob. John bought three ears, which he added to the BBQ. Then he continued further down the row of fine eateries and stopped to buy two roasted turkey legs. After handing them to me, John crossed to the other side of the pathway to a funnel cake stand. He ordered three cakes with cinnamon. Then to wash it all down, he stepped next door to a drink stand, where he talked them into selling him a gallon of tea.

As we started to hunt for a place to sit and eat, we clearly had too much stuff to carry. Finally, we found an empty picnic table and sat down to dig in. Moving that hog worked up my appetite. I inhaled one of the BBQ sandwiches and an ear of corn. I don't know what it is about Rodeo food, but it just tastes soooooooooo good. I sat there patiently while John ate everything else on the table. Apparently, Rodeo food was to his liking as well. As I sat there, I could feel all the bumps and bruises starting to hurt. All of a sudden, I felt like violating a couple of obligations with respect to the big guy sitting across from me. Heck, I started out the day ready to take a nap, and now I was beaten up severely. It was all his fault. All because of a stupid @$$ hog!!

"John, before I get so sore that I can't walk, is there anything you want to talk about to put in the newsletter this month?"

"Yup, I sure do. I have something that has been running around in my head for a while. I have been needing to talk about a goat."

"A goat? What do you mean a goat? I just got through with you and a hog. I don't want to have anything to do with a goat. I am sick of animals right now; just stop it."

John just shook his head sympathetically, gave me a sad look, and continued on.

"You know, Brother Chris, I travel around the State a bit. I sometimes get to see degrees being done by other Lodges. Heck, sometimes I get to work in some of those degrees. Before the degree, the Brothers are out in the fellowship hall eating and socializing. There is always one or more of the Brothers warning the new candidate to watch out for the goat. When I hear that, I just shake my head in sadness. Picture this, here is a man who doesn't know what is going to happen to him. He is most assuredly a little nervous. He has been made to listen to a mandatory reading from the monitor, which asks him to open his heart and mind and receive the light that will be offered to him during his initiation. He is told that there is no horseplay and that the degree is very solemn and serious. Heck, everyone worries when they have to go through an initiation that they will be made to do something demeaning or be made fun of. To hear that everything is serious and without any games is a comfort to that candidate. Then someone walks up to him and asks him if he brought food for the goat and his stress level goes up. When the candidate is going through his degree, we want and need him to listen and absorb the words and lessons presented. Instead, he is thinking about a dang goat."

"I know what you are talking about, Brother John. I have seen it myself. I don't think the Brothers that do it intend for it to be mean, but it has the same effect."

"You're durn right it's mean. You know we don't ride goats or have anything to do with goats in any of the degrees. Did you know that the anti-Masons started the goat, or riding a goat reference, as a way to ridicule our Craft?"

I must have had a surprised look on my face because John said,

"It's true. I read that there were men in England who had been rejected for membership in the Fraternity. They made up stories about Freemasons 'raising the devil and riding on his goat.' Even though it was completely false, it was told over and over by anti-Masons. It really hurt our Fraternity. I also read those early Masons referred to the supreme being as the 'God of all Things.' Once again, those enemies of Masonry used the first letters of those words to spell GOAT. They claimed it was proof positive of their suspicions. Now, we have Brothers who are ignorant of the real meaning of the Masonic Goat. They think it's funny to have a little fun with the candidate by making him think there really is a goat. If these Brothers knew what they were doing to Masonry by continuing this, they might think about not doing it at all."

Then John pulled a folded note out of his pocket and slid it across the table to me.

"Look at what I found in a book that is an anti-Masonic book."

I unfolded it, and there was a picture of a goat on its hind legs with a sinister look on his face and a poem called *When Father Rode the Goat*.

When Father Rode the Goat

The house is full of arnica

And mystery profound;

We do not dare to run about

Or make the slightest sound;

We leave the big piano shut

And do not strike a note;

The doctor's been here seven times

Since father rode the goat.

He joined the lodge a week ago —

Got in at 4 a.m.

And sixteen brethren brought him home

Though he says he brought them.

His wrist WAS sprained and one big rip,

Had rent his Sunday coat —

There must have been a lively time

When father rode the goat.

He's resting on the couch to-day!

And practicing his signs —

The hailing signal, working grip,

And other monkeyshines;

He mutters passwords 'neath his breath,

And other things he'll quote —

They surely had an evening's work

When father rode the goat.

He has a gorgeous uniform,

All gold and red and blue;

A bat with plunges and yellow braid,

And golden badges too.

But, somehow, when we mention it,

He wears a look so grim

We wonder if he rode the goat

Or if the goat rode him.

"Well, that's a cute little poem Brother John, but when you think about it, it's pretty offensive to Masons or should be."

"Exactly my point, Brother. Here we have people bashing Masonry. They have no clue what we do or who we are. Filled with jealousy, fear, or maybe even anger; all they want is to do is tear down our Fraternity. The worst part is that our own Brethren have perpetuated this ridiculous story by using it as a hazing tool."

I just nodded, and he got real quiet. John got a sort of pained look on his face.

"I didn't realize it bothered you as much as it does." John's face changed from pained to more of a constipated look.

"As much as it aggravates me, I just realized that my whole body has just tightened up, the pain is tremendous, and I don't think I can even stand up, much less walk."

"I don't understand Brother John. I'm the one who got hurt the worse. I was dragged; you were riding."

"Riding, my foot," John muttered. "I was bouncing around like a rag doll on top of that monster."

"Well I don't remember seeing you as I had my own problems to worry about," I said, laughing.

"You do look like you've been ridden hard and put up wet." He pointed to my shirt and started chuckling,

"At least I've still got my clothes on."

By then, we were both laughing. I think the people were walking by, thinking we were intoxicated. We laughed at each other's appearance; we looked like 100-year-old men trying to get up and walk. I had to help John up, and he almost fell twice. For some reason that I can't explain, both of us thought it was pretty funny. We must have been a sorry sight walking back to the barn very, very slowly, trying to hold each other up. I left John at the barn leaning against his hog pen.

I told him goodbye and shuffled as best as I could towards the parking lot, trying not to defame John's good name with each step. I just about got to the barn door, and a thought came to mind. I turned and called to John, "Hey John, what is your hog's name anyway?"

He got a real goofy look on his face, shook his head. "You are not going to believe this, but his name is *Jubalum*." I just laughed and turned away—what a perfect name for that mean old hog. I hope I can walk tomorrow.

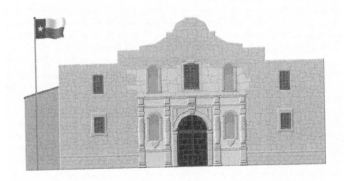

REMEMBER THE ALAMO AND IT'S NOT ALL YOU CAN EAT

It was Friday night, and I was on my way home from work, reflecting on a busy week and looking forward to the weekend. My cell phone rang and when I answered it, there was Big John.

"Hello, Brother!"

"I don't want to even talk to you. It took me almost a week for the soreness to go away. I am going to have to go see a therapist to deal with the hog nightmares I am having."

"Aw, quit yer whining ya big baby," he growled. "You ought to be glad I got you out of your easy chair and gave you something to do."

"I hope you didn't call me to insult me. Before you ask, no, I am not available for any other cockamamie scheme you might be thinking about."

"Enough of the small talk, Brother; do you know what tomorrow is?"

I knew this had to be a trick question, but I was intrigued. "Ok, I'll bite. What is tomorrow?"

"Tomorrow is the 175th anniversary of the fall of the Alamo. Are you going to be there for the Masonic celebration?"

"Ah, well, I have always wanted to go, but I am usually working. I really hadn't thought about it."

"You need to think about it and meet me down there in the morning!" he yelled in my ear.

I didn't even know John was in town, but I agreed to meet him at the designated meeting place behind the Alamo. I got up on Saturday morning and looked out the window; and it was a little cloudy but looked like the start of a nice day. I got ready, and when I stepped outside, I realized it was cold and windy. Since I was wearing a coat and tie, I was not real happy about the wind and temperature. I headed downtown anyway. About halfway there, it started raining, and the temperature hadn't gone up at all. By this point, I said the heck with it and found a place to turn around to head back home. John was just going to have to tell me about what happened. I swear that guy must have a GPS tracker on my truck because as soon as I started back toward home, my phone rang. I looked at the caller ID, and I cringed when I saw it was John.

"Where the heck are you?"

"Headed home, I am chickening out."

"If you don't show up down here, there will be heck to pay," he snarled.

"Look, John, it's raining, the wind is blowing bad, and it is cold out there."

"You need to turn around and get down here," John growled. "The sun is out, the wind has stopped, and it's not raining. Just come on."

I turned around again and made my way downtown. Surprisingly I found a place to park. When the parking meter machine spit out my parking receipt, it promptly disappeared down the street before I could grab it. Yup, you guessed it wind, and lots of it. By the time I worked my way through the crowd of Brother Masons to where John was standing, I was damp from the drizzle, I was cold; and not happy.

"I thought you said it was dry, sunny, and calm down here," I said through clenched teeth.

"Well, it was when I talked to you," John said with an innocent grin.

I looked at all the Brothers on either side of him, and they all shook their heads. I glared back at John, but before I could speak, he pointed at the bag-pipers in their kilts forming up in the middle of the street for the walk over to the Alamo.

John said, "You ought to be glad you aren't one of them. Just pray that a gust of wind doesn't blow them there skirts up. That would ruin a perfect morning."

The procession formed up. We merged with the crowd and walked over to the front of the Alamo behind the Grand Master of Texas and the other Grand Lodge officers, with bagpipes blaring. It was quite a sight of all those Brothers in their Masonic regalia. We were also joined by members of the Shrine Temple and the DeMolay boys. John and I positioned ourselves so that we could see everything going on. After paying our respects to the Supreme Architect of the Universe and our country and state's flags, one of the Brothers gave an inspirational talk about the American Flag. We listened while the Grand Orator introduced officials from the city and from the Daughters of the Republic of Texas. The Orator made some opening remarks about the Alamo and its importance in Texas, wrapping it up with a little American history.

As the Orator was praising the heroes who lost their lives at the Alamo 175 years ago, I heard John's voice next to me. He was talking kind of low, so I leaned in to listen to what he was saying. I heard him slowly saying the names, "James Bonham, Jim Bowie, Juan Seguin, David Crockett, Almaron

Dickenson, William Travis." These were all Brothers who died at the Alamo. I glanced at his face. I saw tears rolling down both cheeks. I guess it could have been because the wind was blowing as hard as it was. Still, I suspect he was, as we all were, thanking those Brothers and the other defenders without whose sacrifice there might not even be a Great State of Texas. Wow, it was sure hard to keep a dry eye thinking about the sacrifices made here.

As I stood there looking up at that beautiful old building, my mind slowly tuned out all the sounds. As my eyes scanned the other Alamo buildings and the area around them in total silence, I could feel the heavyweight of the emotions that this hallowed place invoked. I could almost see the faces of those one hundred and eighty-seven heroes looking down on all of us with smiles of approval and appreciation on their faces. As the lump formed in my throat, I felt so very proud to be an American and a Texan!

I snapped out of my trance in time to hear the Grand Master's address. A final prayer and thanks were given to the brave men who gave their lives for all of us. We walked in silence back to where our vehicles were parked. We were enjoying the feeling of being there. It's almost impossible to stand at the Alamo and not be moved by what it represents. As I reached for my door handle, John informed me that if I didn't feed him soon, he would pass out from malnutrition.

"Come on, John, who's being the baby now? We don't have time for lunch right now because we have to get to the Grand Masters Conference."

"I didn't come down here to go to the conference. I came for the Alamo anniversary."

"Well, you drug me down here for this, so now you have to go with me to the conference. If you don't go, I will give your name to the Grand Master as a Brother who blew off his conference, and you can bet I will do it too."

"Ok, ok, I'll go with you," he whined. "But I am hungry."

I snapped back at him, "don't worry, there's a brunch at the conference, so load it up and let's go."

Well, the brunch did not come close to filling John up. He was eyeballing the other Brothers' plates at our table, so I bought him another plate to hold him over until supper. The conference was excellent. There were around one hundred Brothers who were in attendance. All I could think of is that it was a waste that the Grand Masters words were only going to be heard by less than 10% of all the Masons in the area. Every officer and every Brother of every Lodge should have been there. The important Grand Lodge programs that nine out of ten Masons have no idea exist or what they are were discussed in detail. And when the Grand Master spoke, he delivered a message of getting back to teaching the meanings of the rituals, symbols', and lessons. He focused on the surface meanings and deeper more profound interpretations. He said that we needed to understand what Masonry really is.

The Grand Master pointed out that Masonry is intended to be a philosophy. Proper study will provide the means to answer the three questions that every man has or will ask at some point in his life:

1. Where did I come from?

2. What is my purpose here?

3. Where am I going?

The Grand Master also said that a student of Masonry should always be studious and inquiring about those more profound, more hidden meanings of our Rituals' lessons. I agreed with him completely; as he noted that "when a man is raised to the sublime degree of a Master Mason, he will have acquired a wealth of inspiration. If that newly raised Mason should become a true student of Masonry, it will last him a lifetime."

The Grand Master sadly told us that our West Gate has been wide open and unguarded for too long. Resulting in an alarming number of men being accepted into the Fraternity that would never have been considered if a proper investigation had been performed. He talked of our history and of getting back to our basics, keeping the ritual pure, and the things we need to do to ensure our future. His words were inspirational and really made me think about my Masonic journey, my Lodge, and the Craft's future. I glanced around the room and saw the same feelings in the other Brothers' eyes. Many, including John, were nodding in agreement with our Grand Master.

John leaned over to me and whispered in my ear, "Durn it, Brother Chris, I sure do wish all the Brothers at the last Grand Lodge could have heard this before it closed. Heck, there ain't many Brothers here. If these Brothers are like many of the Brothers at my Lodge, some will pass the words along, and unfortunately, some won't. But every Brother needs to hear this."

"You are right, John, but how are you going to get the word to everyone when they don't show up?"

"I don't know," he growled. "But I will sure give it some deep thought while I'm eating. You are going to feed me, aren't you?"

"You have got to be kidding me, John," I said with a shocked look on my face. "We just ate less than an hour ago."

With a look that conveyed to me that he wasn't kidding at all, John exclaimed, "My stomach has been growling for the last fifteen minutes, and I need to eat something." Actually, I had heard something emanating from his general vicinity that sounded like something a heck of a lot more lethal than a stomach growl.

On the way back downtown to his truck, I tried to think of a place to stop and eat to satisfy his taste buds when he noticed an all-you-can-eat Chinese buffet. He got all excited,

"O' boy, I am in the mood for some good old Chinese food and a lot of it."

I had never been to an all-you-can-eat buffet with John yet, and it struck me as a great deal for John but not for the restaurant. I thought about how in Vegas, they always identify the people who win a lot at cards because they count the cards, so they aren't allowed in the casinos. I got a little chuckle thinking about if the same thing happened to John in his town with the all-you-can-eat buffets.

When we got to our table, John was gone in a flash to the buffet. By the time I got back to the table, he was working on one of two heaping plates of food in front of him. A little Chinese lady walked by and smiled and nodded at both of us. Her gaze seemed to linger on John's double plate, but she smiled and continued on to the other tables. Our drinks came. We sat there enjoying the food, which was excellent. I think John had at least one of everything. I barely finished half of my plate when he was up and heading back for the buffet again. John returned shortly with two more heaping plates full. Out of the corner of my eye, I could see the little Asian lady looking our way again. I figured she must be one of the owners. I don't know why but it made me a bit uneasy. She was way too interested in John and his meal.

Soon John was finished with those two plates and happily on his way back to the buffet for the third time. I was just finishing my first plate as John headed back to our table when it happened. I could see that little Chinese lady making a beeline for our table. Just as John did, she got there, stabbing a long boney finger right into John's chest, and angrily began to talk really fast. Now, she was 4ft 10, and John is 6ft 7, so she had her hand way above her head and looking straight up into his wide-eyed, shocked face, and in a high shrill voice, she let him have it.

"You fat boy. You eat too much. You go home now. You eat up all profits!"

She reached up and took the plates from his hands, turned him around, and proceeded to herd him toward the door pushing him in the back every couple of steps. I would have helped him if I had not been choking on my tea laughing so hard. All the other diners were staring with disbelief as this tiny lady ran this huge guy out the door, giving him a tongue lashing every step of the way. Just before they got to the door, one of the other employees intercepted them. He started talking to the lady, waving their hands at each other and gesturing toward a very quiet and scared-looking John Deacon.

Our waitress had come over to me and began apologizing, but I told her this was the most fun I had had in a long time. Finally, I said to her that I would pay for two more plates if it would get my Brother a reprieve. She smiled and went to the door to deliver the word. As soon as the older lady heard, she immediately stopped talking and began smiling, grabbed John's hand, escorted him back to the table, and sat him down. She then retreated amid a lot of bowing and smiling.

I looked across the table at a visibly shaken John who shook his head, "What the heck just happened?"

I laughed, "Well, I think you just got yourself whupped upon by an 85-pound Chinese lady. You better get to eating before she changes her mind." Tentatively he began to eat again.

Soon John was satisfied that all heck would not break loose again. The rest of the diners finally stopped looking our way, and everything went back to normal. Not surprisingly, he got done pretty quickly and was ready to leave. I handed him the bill, which he gladly took, and headed to the cashier. After John paid, he turned around to leave, and the older Chinese lady was standing right behind him. It startled him. I thought he would have a heart attack, but she smiled at him and shook his hand and bowed at him about ten times. John bowed back as he was backing out the door. I told him how ridiculous he looked, and he reminded me that it probably was not a good idea to turn his back on her. I agreed.

We piled in my truck and headed out. It was a short drive without any conversation. I pulled up to John's truck, but instead of getting out, John just sat there staring straight ahead out the window. I was going to ask what the matter was but decided instead to be patient. I figured he would let it out when he was ready. It didn't take long.

John took a deep breath and in a soft voice, "Brother Chris, he is right, you know... everything he said is right."

I figured he was talking about our Grand Master, but instead of asking and being wrong, I kept my big mouth shut and let him talk. I had to lean over a little bit cause he was still talking kinda low.

"We really don't do a very good job of investigating men who want to join the Fraternity. I have seen it all. I have seen Brothers sign a petition for a man who just walked into the Lodge off the street. I have seen Brothers mark on a petition that they have known the man for months and even years when they only just met. I have seen Brothers investigate a potential candidate in the Fellowship Hall of the Lodge before a meeting just so he could turn in the report on time. I have seen Brothers meet potential candidates in restaurants to investigate instead of at the candidate's home. I have seen candidates be investigated and been voted to receive the Mysteries without their wives even knowing about it. I have seen too many times all three investigators meeting with a prospective candidate at the same time for the investigation. I have even seen Brothers fill out the investigation form before meeting with the applicant. I have seen all these things and more. All in the name of quantity and not quality. It's enough to make you sick just thinking about it."

I shrugged slightly. John continued as he got a little louder.

"Do you know what it has gotten us? I'll tell you exactly what it has gotten us. It has gotten us men of questionable character. Men who, if we had really done a proper investigation, would never have been admitted among us. We have men whose only reason for joining is because they thought it would help them in business. We have men whose only desire to be initiated is to **See What the Heck it is All About** with no intention or desire to truly become a Mason. Oh, and there have been and continue to be many whose only desire is to clean up or enhance their tarnished reputations by becoming a Mason in name only. Even those who join just to join because that's what they do, they join everything. You know there is a reason why the question about belonging to other organizations is on the petition. Most of the aforementioned individuals drop out as soon as they realize that Masonry does not and will not feed their fraud and deception.

But how much wasted time and damage to our Fraternity is done by these misguided souls? How many lies noted on the petition could have been revealed if only a proper investigation had been done? How many hours wasted by degree teams and mentors and instructors on these liars and cheats? How many good and true Masons have been disillusioned by the admission of those unqualified and unworthy to ever be taken by the hand as a Brother? I think that it is impossible to calculate.

Sometimes it seems that we are afraid of turning someone down. Why is that? I often wonder, knowing what I know about what true Masonry is, why there are not lines of good men wanting to become Masons. Could it be that there is a perception that Masonry and Masons aren't as pure as they are supposed to be? How much Masonic good will be destroyed by these imposters and pretenders. I shudder to consider. Brother Chris, what makes Masonry pure is what will make Masonry grow always and forever. We have been so blinded by declining membership we have begun to sow the seeds of our total demise. I don't know how I could state it any plainer than that."

"Brother John, you said a mouthful right there, and I know it's all true," I noted the sadness in his eyes. "We Masons are responsible for this, and we Masons have to stop it now."

We shook hands and made a silent vow to make sure to do what needed to be done to correct this problem. I could see John was deeply bothered, so I walked around the truck as he got out and gave my sad-eyed Brother a hug and said, "Don't worry, my Brother, we will get it going."

John smiled, "I know we will; we have to."

And with that, he climbed up into Ol' Blackie, waved, and roared off in a cloud of black smoke. When I stopped coughing, I made a mental note to get him in to change those fuel filters next month.

To all my Brothers out there:

Is it worth it to you that only admitted are those who are duly and truly prepared, worthy, and well qualified?

It should be.

THE KARAOKE KING, BEING MADE OR BECOMING

It was a Friday evening right at 6 PM, and I was locking the shop's door when I heard a diesel truck pull in behind me. Before I could turn around, that familiar melodious voice floated across the parking lot to my ears.

"Hey Brother Chris, where do you think you are going? I've got some serious truck problems."

"Well, you are just S.O.L., my Brother. There's no one here that can fix it until Monday."

He got a shocked look on his face, "Yes, John I said you're S.O.L. Do you know what that stands for?"

"Of course, I know what your saying. It stands for Sorry, Out of Luck. But in my neck of the woods the 'S' stands for something else."

"I guess we are lucky that we aren't in your neck of the woods then. What's wrong with your truck? It sounds good to me."

"Awww, there's nothing wrong with Ol' Blackie. I was just giving you a hard time. Actually, I have a pretty serious meeting with the owner of my company tomorrow morning. It might not be a good one," he said as his grin turned into a frown. "They are doing a lot of cutbacks because of the economy, and it might just be my turn. I will know tomorrow. It's not going to be easy to sleep tonight."

I felt terrible for him and naturally I wanted to help. I told him that I had an obligation to work that night at a Fiesta event in San Antonio called Night in Old San Antonio, better known as NIOSA. It's a big yearly party here in San Antonio, and John had never been so I invited him along. I knew it would take his mind off the next day, so I loaded him up, and we headed downtown to Fiesta. Now Fiesta is a big deal in San Antonio. It is an eleven-day and night party of carnivals, parades, picnics, and more kinds of food than you can imagine. I have worked it for the past 20 years at what they call Night in Old San Antonio, four nights of fun, food, and really happy people. My softball buddies and I work the souvenir booth in Clown Alley. People come from all over the world to Fiesta in San Antonio, and it's always a lot of fun. I thought John could eat all he wanted and be around a lot of happy people; most of them would be slightly too inebriated. I figured this would be perfect for John.

Little did I know how perfect it would be for him. The night started out calmly enough. I introduced John to the team, and he jumped right in selling t-shirts and all kinds of flashing souvenirs. After about 20 minutes, I saw him sniffing the air. I could tell his production was going to go down quickly if I didn't feed him soon. We joined the mass of party-goers who were hopping from food booth to food booth, trying as many different things as possible. I told John that we would hit a few places and then go back to our booth and eat. Right around the corner from our booth was what they called Fat Bread, a kind of English Muffin with a layer of cheese topped by a layer of mushrooms heated up. I told John it was one of my favorites; he got four. I shook my head and told him to be mindful that there was a lot of different food to try. He nodded in understanding, and we dove back into the crowd to find the next food booth. About 50 feet down, we encountered a booth selling Bratwurst and Sauerkraut, which I was going to pass up, but John nearly jerked me off my feet when he reached out to stop me.

"I love German Brats and Kraut!"

"OK, get some, and let's go."

Pretty soon, we were back in the flow. By the time we got back to our booth, we had stopped at least 10 different food booths. John managed to buy three different kinds of meatballs, some nachos, two different types of gorditas, a turkey leg, some fried green tomatoes, a couple of corn dogs, and Matinee chips like big fried jalapenos. He really got excited about a booth with steer on a Stick. I think John got 4 or 5 of those too. I stayed a little ahead of him the whole time, so I wouldn't have to foot the bill for the double armload of gastric distress that he was carrying around. When we finally got back to our booth, I laid my stuff out and motioned to a spot for John to sit down. I looked to see all the food he had bought, but all he had in his hands was empty containers and wrappers.

"What happened to all your food John?"

"Heck, Brother Chris, I was so hungry I was eating as we were walking. Now I ate all of it, and I am hungry again."

"If you want to fight that crowd again, then have at it, but I am going to eat now."

"I have to get some more of that steer on a stick and some more of those jalapenos. Oh, and I saw a couple of other things I wanted, so I will be back in a little while."

Before I could reply, he was gone. I was pretty happy to just sit there and enjoy some of the tastiest food that is only available once a year at Fiesta.

The only negative, the booth next to ours was a Karaoke booth. Hour after agonizing hour, there was a constant assault to the musical sensibilities of anyone within a 50 ft radius of that booth. I didn't think it was possible to butcher good music. I finished up eating and went back to selling t-shirts. A few minutes later John returned to the booth. He seemed like a different person. He was happy and grinning at everyone like a big goofus. John had all the girls in the booth giggling and laughing. I can't swear to it, but I think he may have encountered a Margarita or two while he was wandering about all by himself, even though he denied it.

All was going good, and business was brisk. I was in a t-shirt selling zone. The next thing I know, my focus was directed to the intro music to one of my favorite songs coming from the karaoke booth. I braced myself for the inevitable off-key, intoxicated version of a great George Strait song. George is a darn good country-western singer in the rest of the world, but in San Antonio, he is the KING. I said a silent apology to the country music Gods as the music paused and the words came............

"Amarillo by morning.... Up from San Antone............ Everything that I got......... Is just what I've got on" ....

Almost immediately, I realized this guy was good. The voice was a little lower than George's but still really good.

"When that sun is high in that Texas sky.... I'll be buckin 'at the County fair....... Amarillo by morning...... Amarillo, I'll be there."

Everyone at the booth thought so too because they were all looking to the right trying to get a look at the singer. I could see a crowd of people had slowed down to hear the song. I had to walk over to the end of the counter to see where the singer was, but all the helpers in the booth were blocking me.

"They took my saddle in Houston .... Broke my leg in Santa Fe .... Lost my wife and a girlfriend.... Somewhere along the way."

I finally nudged one of my buddies out of the way. I just about fainted.

"I'll be looking for eight when they pull that gate, and I hope that judge ain't blind."

It was John. I never saw John leave the booth.

"Amarillo by morning...... Amarillo is on my mind."

By now, all of our customers had left our booth, and all the surrounding booths were also empty. The crowd that had slowed was now at a dead stop. They were all bunched up in front of the karaoke booth. Well, I wasn't the only one who was standing there with my mouth hanging open. The crowd that was getting bigger by the minute was really enjoying the performance. And on he went.

"Amarillo by morning....... Up from San Antone......... Everything that I got... is just what I've got on" ....

All I could do is shake my head and smile.

"I ain't got a dime, but what I got is mine... I ain't rich, but Lord, I'm free........."

All my buddies were looking at me like, who is this guy?

"Amarillo by morning....... Amarillo's where I'll be."

All I could do is shrug my shoulders and wait for the finish.

"Amarillo by morning, Amarillo's where I'll be."

The crowd let out a big cheer causing a big goofy grin to appear on John's face. They started chanting more, more, but I think that was the only song John knew. He came down the stairs to the street level. As he walked, everyone wanted to shake his hand, and he had more friends right then than he knew what to do with. He was soaking it all up, shaking hands with the men, and hugging the ladies. The guys in our booth had their arms extended above their heads and were bowing to him (I think they all had too much to drink), letting him know how much they enjoyed it. I couldn't believe it when I saw him giving autographs to a couple of over-partied women. People were trying to hand him all different kinds of adult beverages, to which he kept declining. I could see that he was overwhelmed and was looking for a way out. I waded out in the middle of the mob and grabbed his arm, and led him back into our booth. He received hugs and high fives from all the workers that should have been selling t-shirts.

I heard our head coach yell for everyone to get back to work. As we turned, I could see people lined up at our booth as far as you could see. They all wanted to buy something and then have John sign it. Some wanted to buy only from John, and others just wanted to shake his hand. It was absolutely ridiculous. The thought of these people waking up tomorrow morning wondering who the heck wrote on their t-shirts gave me a couple of chuckles. As much as John was enjoying it made it worth it. It didn't take long before we were sold out of all our products. We closed the booth, and the crowd finally went back to passing by. John flopped down on the bench, looking exhausted.

"Where the heck did you learn how to sing like that, Brother John? I wouldn't have thought you had it in you."

His eyes narrowed as he growled back at me, "Brother Chris, there are a multitude of things you don't know about me. I have talents even I don't know about yet."

With a totally blank look on my face, "I don't know what to say to that, John, but you did good."

John softly said, "Apparently, all those years of my Mom dragging us kids to church and making us sing in the choir paid off." We all nodded in agreement. "I do believe that I have had about as much fun in one night as a man should be allowed to have. Take me home, Brother Chris."

We shook hands all around, and we headed for my truck. He looked awful tired. "If you hadn't had that Margarita or whatever it was that you had, would you have had the nerve to get up there and sing?"

"I had been thinking about singing after hearing all the bad singing that was going on, and I just felt like it," he said defensively.

"Yeah, right." John lapsed into silence on the trip to his hotel. We didn't speak on the way to his hotel. I could tell John was thinking about his meeting.

I followed him up to his room to make sure he got there OK. I thought he would complain about it, but he didn't. When John asked me to come in to tell me something, I didn't complain either. He sat down on the edge of the bed. I took the chair across from him. After about a minute, he looked up.

"You know, I drive around a lot and all over Texas. I have a lot of time to think. I was thinking the other day about the one topic that you see written about more than anything else is, what is Masonry? Everyone gets all caught up in the definition of Masonry. It gets confusing reading all the dozens and dozens of different definitions of our Fraternity. Everyone is writing about what it is and what it's not, and they are all saying pretty much the same dang thing, just using different fancy words. Sometimes I spend 15 or 20 minutes looking through the dictionary just to get definitions of the words used in their description of Masonry. It doesn't take much of that to get a simple country boy confused and frustrated."

He paused and let out a big yawn. I tried as hard as possible to keep from doing the same.

"Masonry is not that complicated, Brother Chris. I know what Masonry is, and I realize that my definition doesn't have a lot of fancy smancy words. Still, when you shake off all the hoity-toity-ness, Masonry is just good instead of bad. It is right instead of wrong, happiness instead of sadness. It is love instead of hate and truth instead of lies. It is light instead of dark. It is caring instead of indifference, and it is order instead of confusion. It is beauty in every way possible, and Masonry, like the soul within all of us, will never, never, never die."

He stopped suddenly, just staring ahead. I didn't know if he was through or not, but I had known him long enough to not assume that he was. I was thinking so intently about what he had said that I didn't that he had laid down on the bed. What an excellent way that was to describe our gentle Fraternity. My concentration was suddenly broken by John's voice.

"This is what Masonry is to me, Brother Chris, and knowing that makes me a better man every day. I want you to know that I decided to become a Mason 35 years ago, and the day I did, my life changed for the good. I was made a Mason 45 years ago. Think about that…and thanks for taking me with you tonight. I had a great time."

I was smiling and nodding until he said he was made a Mason 45 years ago. Now I was confused big time. I noticed John laid his head back on the pillow.

"Brother John, I enjoyed spending time with you tonight too, and I …John, are you asleep?"

I stood up to get a better look at his face, and sure enough, he was out like a light. I grabbed the other end of the bedspread and threw it over him. Before I got to the door, he was loudly sawing logs.

"Pleasant dreams, Brother John," I called out as I slid the door shut. "Good luck in your meeting tomorrow." I am not sure, but I still think he sneaked a couple of Margaritas before he decided to become a country singer. And darn him anyway! Now I had to figure out the difference between being "made" a Mason and "becoming" a Mason.

If y'all figure it out, please let me know.

PEANUTS ON THE FLOOR AND THE WISDOM OF BROTHER BILL

You know how sometimes when you are working, doing chores, and someone will pop into your mind, and shortly after that, that person comes walking in through the door? Well, it happened to me last week. I was at work, and all of a sudden, Big John popped into my mind. I tried really hard to put him out of my mind, but he wouldn't leave …… Ha! Kind of like when John is here in person. Anyway, I was wondering about what happened between him and his boss last month. I remembered that he was worried about their meeting. I sure hoped he didn't get laid off because his job was the only reason he came down our way every month. What was I going to do if he didn't show up every month? As I was mulling over the pros and the cons of that scenario, the front door flew open, and there he was.

"Helloooooooo Fellers," he bellowed with his arms spread wide like he was addressing his subjects. "It is I, your Brother John. I can go no further. I must eat."

Roger looked over at me and said, "I think he is looking for you. Would you be so kind to let your friend know that he's scaring all the customers."

"Yes. John did you hear that? Don't yell so loud; you're scaring all the customers."

"Oh man, I'm sorry," John apologized as he looked around quickly. "Hey, wait a minute….. there's no customers in here."

I guess that answered my question about his meeting with his boss last month. He was way too happy for a man who had been laid off from his job.

"Well if there were any customers, you sure would have scared them. I was actually just thinking about you. So, what happened at your meeting last month? I was a little worried about you."

"Brother Chris, you are not going to believe this. My boss wanted to tell me what a good job I was doing, and the conversation changed to him asking me about becoming a Mason. He said that when I talk about the Lodge and being a Mason, he can tell how proud I am to be one. He said it seems to be the source of all my energy."

"I could have told him that was wrong," I butted in sarcastically. "The source of your energy is all that food you eat."

"I am not even going to dignify that with a response," giving me a cold stare. Out of the corner of my eye, I could see Roger with his head down laughing as silently as he could.

"I'm serious, Brother; when my boss said that to me, I told him that the energy actually comes from a higher source. That energy, along with the principles and teachings in Masonry, makes me the man I am today. Brother Chris, it's a good feeling when someone wants to be a Mason because of who you are."

I had lost the sarcasm, and I noticed that Roger had stopped laughing. I could tell Roger liked what John said. "Brother John, that is good; I have to agree with your boss."

"Well, now that you are done being a smart alec. Take me to eat before I have to get violent. I have a lot to tell you."

"OK, OK, calm down. I am going to take you to Texas Road House."

"I have never been there before. How about you quit talking, and let's go!"

We showed up at a bad time because the place was packed. Several people were waiting for tables. We ended up only having to wait about 10 minutes before we were escorted to a booth. All the way to the table, John was checking out all the peanut shells on the floor. He made a comment to the hostess as we were sitting down that somebody ought to do some sweeping up. She smiled sweetly and informed him that there were peanuts in the buckets on the table, and he was allowed to throw the shells on the floor. I didn't think it was that big of a deal, but John was like a kid in a candy store. He grabbed a handful of peanuts out of the bucket and began popping them open and eating them one after another. After each shell was empty, he ceremoniously flipped it out and watched its travel path all the way to the floor. John soon realized that having a mouthful of nuts and nothing to wash them down with is not a good thing. He began to frantically look around for a server and finally began waving wildly, hoping to attract someone's attention. I could tell that his actions had annoyed the two ladies in the booth behind us. I waved at them and apologized as our waiter stopped in front of our table and announced he was going to be our server.

I noticed that his badge identified him as Tony, the store manager. He introduced himself and apologized for the wait. He explained that they were swamped because two servers had not shown up for their shift, so he had to fill in. John was trying unsuccessfully to push out some words, but all I heard was gibberish. His face was getting red, and he was staring at me with disgust in his eyes.

"Hi Tony. I think he has had too many nuts and needs something to drink." Immediately John began nodding and grunting in agreement. "Can we get two ice teas please?"

It didn't take long before Tony reappeared at our table. John was still staring bullets at me. John grabbed his tea and gulped down about half of the glass before he paused to take a breath. Tony watched him with amused indifference and asked if we were ready to order, to which I said we were. He asked if it would be on one or two tickets, and simultaneously John and I pointed at each other.

Tony rolled his eyes, "Figure it out, guys. I don't have all day." I started to think that I didn't like Tony's attitude, considering he didn't know how much money this table was about to make him.

"Wait a minute, Brother Chris, I paid for all my stuff last month at the Fiesta."

"Yeah, but the month before, I had to pay the Chinese lady for two extra meals so that she would stop yelling at you."

John looked at me for a few seconds, then at Tony, "It ain't fair, but I guess I am buying this month."

I quickly ordered the T-Bone steak salad with extra ranch dressing. I was hoping that John would decide quickly that way Tony could go help someone else.

John, still looking at the menu, finally looked up, "I'll have two of them T-Bone steak salads. Then I will have that Porter house steak cooked medium well, and don't even think about bringing it out here bleeding all over the place. Put a baked potato next to it with all the fixins you can find. Bring us some of those good-smelling rolls before the smell drives me crazy. One more thing there pardner, can you fill up this here bucket of peanuts?"

Tony was shaking his head in disbelief as he turned towards the kitchen.

"I sure do like these peanuts, Brother Chris," as John grabbed another handful.

Tony brought a full bucket and took away the empty one that John finished. As we were waiting for our lunches, we made small talk about the weather, the price of gas, and such. I noticed a good-sized pile of peanut shells building up next to our table. I could hear the loud crunching of shells as people passed our booth. Pretty soon, our lunch arrived. Three people to carry it all, and as usual, John's plates took up most of the table.

John lapsed into his usual silence while he was eating, which was OK with me. One of the best things about that T-Bone steak salad is that they put two hard-boiled eggs cut in half in it. That is one of my favorite parts, after the steak, of course. It always amazes me how fast John can finish off a meal. I was about halfway done with my salad when John finished both of his and attacked the other steak and baked potato. He had just asked for three more rolls.

I noticed John was eyeballing something intently behind me over my shoulder. I asked him what he was looking at, and John said that a strange-looking guy was sitting at another table. I turned in my seat to look, but nobody looked strange to me. When I turned back around I told John I didn't see anyone weird. He just shrugged and continued chewing. I looked down at my salad, and I had a strange feeling that I was missing one of my eggs. I looked up at John, then back at my plate, then back at John. His face remained expressionless, still chewing away. Out of the corner of my eye, I saw a lady at the table next to us trying not to laugh. I stared at John again, and his expression never changed. I really wasn't sure, but I was not going to turn around again.

I kept a close eye on John until I finished my salad. Shortly after that, John finished, to my surprise, he went back to the peanuts. Holy moly, I wonder if he has ever gotten filled up! I waited patiently to hear what important stuff he had to tell me, and finally, as if he just remembered what it was, John started talking.

"Brother Chris, I got to do something last weekend that I never thought I would get to do. I went to a different Lodge to confer an Entered Apprentice degree. The candidate was my nephew, Travis."

"*Wow*, John, that sounds great. How did it go?"

"It was really great. It was just a couple of months ago that my nephew told me he wanted to become a Mason, and he turned in a petition. As he was going through the process, I contacted the Lodge Secretary, Brother Guido, and let him know I wanted to come down for the degree. Brother Guido had kept me in the loop on what was going on. Once they got all the investigating, voting, and all that stuff done, they got it scheduled for a Saturday morning. That worked out great because I didn't have to miss any work. I stopped being nervous about working in Degrees a long time ago, and I had never conferred a degree in a different Lodge before. The fact that it was my nephew and at a Lodge that I had never visited made me nervous as heck and excited at the same time. I didn't even sleep the night before. I was worried that the alarm clock in my hotel wouldn't go off on time, and

I would miss the whole dang thing. That is too much stress for an old guy like me."

"So did it go off on time?"

"*Well, Gol Durn it Brother Chris, of course, it did,*" John growled. "I am telling you about it, ain't I? Anyway, I picked up Travis, and we got to the Lodge around 7:30 AM. Ohhhh my gosh, Brother Chris, you should see this Lodge. It's an old Lodge which was established in the 1870s. It's got an alley running down one side of it and the local newspaper office on the other side. This building has to be a hundred years old or better. When I opened the door, the wonderful smell of bacon and sausage cooking in the frypan, biscuits baking in the oven, and freshly brewed coffee hit me like a freight train.... a real good freight train." John had a big smile. "I know this will be hard for you to believe Brother Chris, but I had clean forgot that I hadn't eaten breakfast."

I looked at John sideways, "Yeah, right, who do you think you are talking to?"

"It's the truth," John whined.

"Anyway, Brother Guido and Brother Paul were in the kitchen. I met them first. Sitting in the dining room waiting to make the gravy for the biscuits was Brother Tom. Brother Tom is the one who checked to make sure I was who I said I was. I met the other three Brothers, Jake, Jeff, and Robert, who were sitting waiting for breakfast. Brother George, one of their new Entered Apprentice's wife, and son were also there. I have to tell you he was one of the most energetic Brothers I have ever seen.

They were all taking turns chastising Brother Guido and Brother Paul about their cooking skills. I learned a big lesson from my Mother when I was a kid that you don't ever criticize the cook; if you plan on eating, that is. So I just kept my mouth shut. Actually, they were giving back as much abuse as they were getting. The friendly ragging on each other was about what you would expect when you get a bunch of Brothers together for work. About that time, three really good-looking ladies came in."

"Ladies? Wait a minute, John, what were the ladies doing there?" I was obviously irritating him.

"*There you go, interrupting me all the time.* Well, if you must know Brother Chris, these ladies happen to be a little partial to me. It was my wife and my two nieces, one of whom was Travis's wife. The Lodge, which I thought was a real nice gesture, invited his family to have breakfast with us. We introduced them all around.

Not long after they arrived, Brother Tom made the gravy, and we all lined up to fill our plates. I think that was one of the best meals I have ever had at Lodge before. Somebody must have told them that I am a growing boy, and I need a lot to keep me going cause they sure made plenty.

After breakfast, all the ladies and kids left. I wandered into the Lodge Room to kinda get the lay of the land, so to speak. I talked with a couple of the other Brothers who were getting the Lodge ready for the degree. Brother Dennis, the Senior Warden introduced himself and explained that he was proteming for the Worshipful Master. He asked me if I was ready to go. I told him I was and sat myself down in the South towards the front of the Lodge Room. I sat there going over the work in my mind.

A couple of minutes later, I looked up. Some Brothers were escorting an older Brother into the Lodge. They sat him down next to me. Before I could say anything, he turned and held out his hand and introduced himself as Brother Bill. I took his hand, and we exchanged that *familiar grip*. I told him who I was. He then asked me a strange question, 'So you're the one.'

I asked him what he meant, and he said he had heard that a Brother from another Lodge was going to confer the degree. He welcomed me and told me that he hadn't been to Lodge for a while. He was glad to be back. He explained that he was almost totally blind and could only see shapes but not faces. I told him it was no problem and that I was right next to him if he needed anything. We both sat back, waiting for the officers to get to their places and get ready to open the Lodge.

All of a sudden, Brother Bill started talking. I turned my head towards him, and he was looking straight ahead, talking in a voice low enough that I had to lean in towards him to hear. He said that he was 85 years old and that he was raised when he was 21. He mentioned that some of the greatest times of his life were sitting in Lodge next to his Dad. Sometimes when he sits in Lodge, he gets a feeling that his Dad is sitting right beside him.

Oh my gosh, Brother Chris, when he said that, a big ol' lump jumped right up in my throat. I was trying my darndest to talk, but nothing would come out."

I knew what he meant because one had just formed in my throat.

"Brother Chris, I swallowed a couple of times, and without really thinking about it, I leaned forward and looked at the empty seat on the other side of him. Then I sat back and leaned over to him and whispered in his ear, 'I think I do see him sitting right there next to you, Brother Bill.' Well, Bill got a big smile on his face, closed his eyes, nodded, and laid his hand on the armrest of the chair next to him. It was all I could do to keep from getting choked up, Brother Chris. Still, luckily, I didn't have time to think about it too much because the gavel came down.

The Worshipful Master began to open the Lodge. As soon as Brother Robert got the door, tiled Brother Tom gave us a prayer, and we were open and ready to go. The Worshipful Master asked the Degree team to take their places, and as I took my place in the East, I looked around the room. Brother J.D. was at the Secretary's desk, ready for me to get it going. Brother Dennis had gone to the West. Brother Scott was in the South. My new Buddy, Brother Guido, was ready to take charge of the candidate as Senior Deacon. Brother John was holding down the Junior Deacons chair, and I could see Brother Robert playing with some kind of coin, ready to do his part. I couldn't see Brother Jeff, but I knew he was with Travis outside the door.

Well, I took a deep breath and dropped the gavel, and we commenced to put on what turned out to be a heck of an Entered Apprentice degree. The guys from the Lodge did an outstanding job. I was awful proud to be there with them. You know you always want the new candidate to get a good degree, but I can tell you for sure that my nephew got a great degree. Brother Cecil gave an excellent Lecture, and Brother Skylar wrapped it all up with the charge.

When I got back to my seat next to Brother Bill, he leaned in and told me that we all did a good job. I thanked him. The Worshipful Master congratulated our new Brother Travis and asked Brother Tom to go over the Lodge protocol. Brother Dennis then asked the Brothers to all stand, give whatever advice and information they would like to give their new Brother. One by one, we all stood and offered congratulations and encouragement as well as helpful advice to Brother Travis. When it was

Brother Bill's turn, he stood and faced the new Brother and welcomed him to the Lodge. With as much emotion as I have ever seen from a Brother in a Lodge, Brother Bill told Brother Travis that he had just made the best decision he would ever make and to not waste what he was given. Then it was my turn. I congratulated Brother Travis and told him that I was proud of him. I told the Worshipful Master and all the Brethren that I was honored to be a part of their degree team, and I thanked them for their hospitality.

The last to speak was the Worshipful Master, Brother Dennis, but to ask questions and learn what the words meant. Then he allowed Brother Travis to speak. He thanked the Lodge for the opportunity to become a Mason and be a member of the Lodge. He thanked the Brothers for taking time on a Saturday to work on his degree. The Worshipful Master then promptly closed the Lodge. Everyone came over to congratulate our new Brother. I took a deep breath, and suddenly I realized that I was tired, really, really tired. I was ready for a nap. But we had to take care of the critical stuff first... lunch."

"Sounds like you had a pretty great weekend, Brother John."

"It sure meant a lot to me to be there for Brother Travis's degree. But to have the opportunity to confer the degree is something I will always be proud of and grateful to the Lodge for. I am looking forward to going back for his other degrees."

I had been concentrating on John's story and didn't notice that Tony was standing at the edge of our table. He had a different kind of smile on his face and said to John, "I hope you don't mind, but I overheard most of your story, and it was a good one." With that, he laid the bill down on the table.

John reached for it, saying, "How much are all those peanuts I ate?"

Tony laughed and told him that they were no charge to customers. While John paid, I took a quick trip to the restroom. When I got back, John was sliding out of the booth.

As we neared the door, a voice called out, "Mr. Deacon?" We turned around, and Tony held out one of those buckets that hold the peanuts on the tables. He handed it to John, "Here's a bucket to carry all your peanuts."

I looked at John with a puzzled look; with his face turning red, he started pulling handfuls of peanuts out of his pants pockets and shirt pockets. Heck, he even had some in both hip pockets.

"Oh my God, John. What are you doing with all these nuts?"

"Well, Tony said I could take all I wanted, so I was just taking some to munch on while I was driving down the road."

As I watched, John darn near filled that bucket with all he pulled out of his pockets. John tried to hand Tony the bucket full of nuts, but he said with a smile, "The bucket is yours to carry the nuts in. Come back and eat here again sometime. Good luck with your nephew."

It struck me then that Tony had been standing at our table longer than I realized. He held out his hand, and John shook it.

John got a big smile on his face, "Thank you young man. We will be back!"

We got to my truck first. I told John I would see him next month and lunch would be on me. As John and his bucket of nuts walked away, I commented that the scene at the door was kind of weird.

John turned, "As it turns out, Tony the manager is Brother Tony."

"How did you know?"

John rolled his eyes and gave me a sideways look. Then it came to me, "Ahhhhh, it must have been that *special grip*."

John smiled and nodded.

Nurse Mona and Are We All Brothers?

Almost the whole month had gone by, and I realized I hadn't heard from the huge one; Brother John. It was almost lunchtime on a Friday, and I thought it would be a real problem if I didn't get to experience the profundity of his wisdom and knowledge. Nahhh, not really. It would mean I would have to make something up, and I surely don't think all of you want to read something I made up.

I called John's cell phone, and after ringing ten times, Mrs. Deacon answered. I thought that it was strange that he wasn't out on the road somewhere. I asked where the great one was, and she told me that he was in the hospital. This scared the heck out of me. Without finding out what was wrong, I calmly assumed that it was bad (we all know what happens when you assume). I asked for the hospital's name, the room number, and hung up. Being a Friday afternoon, we were winding down for the week. We had a few cars needing to be picked up by customers, so I asked Leonard if I could get out a little early to visit John in the hospital. He wanted to know what was wrong with John, and all I could do is stand there with a dumb look on my face and say, "I don't know." He said it's probably not good at his age, so get out of here and call us and let us know.

I knew I had a long drive ahead of me, but getting out at noon would put me at the hospital in plenty of time for visitors. I drove as fast as I dared and pulled up in front of the hospital right at five o'clock. It wasn't a big hospital, but I still ended up having to ask for directions anyway. They had him ensconced in a room on the second-floor way back in the corner (big surprise). I could hear his booming voice long before I got to his door. It sounded like he was complaining about something (another big surprise).

As I got to the doorway, I saw Mrs. Deacon kiss him on the cheek and tell him to behave himself. She looked up and saw me standing in the doorway. She quickly came over to greet me and said, "I am glad you are here. I have to run some errands. You can deal with the grouch for a while."

I promised I would get him under control, to which she gave me a little smirk on her way out the door. As I stepped into the room, a nurse flew by me, blocked my way, and snarled. "Only immediate family is allowed in here."

Before I could reply, John said, "He's OK, he's my Brother. Please let him by."

She walked up to me, and I could see the little badge around her neck that read, *Hi, my name is Mona. I am here to give you the best care anywhere.*

While I was contemplating that, she looked me up and down with a stern stare. "You don't look a bit like him."

With no time to think, I quickly replied, "We had different mothers."

She continued her inspection and walked out of the room, mumbling something about "that's what they all say."

I shook my head to clear it, walked over to John's bed, and asked him what he was in for. He said that they were going to do a knee replacement the next day. I was stunned. I spoke with a trace of sarcasm in my voice, "I drove all the way up here, worried about you and all that's wrong is the bum knee you have had forever?"

"My wife told me you hung up before she could tell you what was going on," he shot back. "It's not my fault you came all the way up here."

"Heck, you could have called me back."

"I told her not to call you back. I am glad you came because otherwise, we couldn't have talked this month, and you would have just had to make something up."

Hmmmm, I thought. *That's a little freaky and way too clairvoyant for me, but John was right.* I settled down in the recliner next to his bed.

"So, what is your major problem? I could hear you complaining about something when I stepped out of the elevator way down the hall. You know they will throw you out of here if you keep it up, and Nurse Mona looks like she could do just that."

"Brother Chris, it's the food. It's terrible, there's not near enough of it, and Nurse Mona doesn't seem to care. I see her and my wife talking in the hall, whispering to each other and looking at me. I think they are doing this to me on purpose. I am about to pass out from hunger."

"OK, OK, John, I will go and get you a big hamburger or something and smuggle it into the hospital. Would that make you happy?"

John's voice got really low, and he looked from side to side like he thought the room might be bugged and whispered, "I have got it handled. We should have some more company in a few minutes."

No sooner than he had uttered those words, four guys walked into the room. One had a bouquet of flowers, one had a card, and the other two were carrying a huge box with a big bow on it. Before anyone could say anything, Nurse Mona appeared in the doorway and announced that only immediate family could be in the room. John told her that all four were his Brothers.

"No way," Nurse Mona said as she proceeded to study each of their faces one by one. They were all frozen in place and obviously afraid to move. She was pretty intimidating. Finally, she turned to John and said, "Mr. Deacon, I see no family resemblance in any of these men."

The gentleman holding the flowers said, "That's because...." and before he could finish, she turned on him and cut him off.

"You'd better not say that you all had different mothers." We all just stood there like statues, all of us afraid to speak. Suddenly, Nurse Mona threw up her hands, "Just be warned that visiting hours are over at eight o'clock, and anyone who is left I will throw out."

I don't know about the other fellers, but I surely believed her and made a note to myself to be long gone by eight o'clock. As she was leaving, John called out to her and asked if she would shut the door because we had some important family business to discuss. She whirled around in the doorway and gave all of us a withering stare which spoke volumes about what she was thinking right then. She backed out, slowly closing the door as she stared deep into our souls.

"Holy Maloney, John, that lady is all business."

"You darn tootin' Brother Chris," John hurriedly replied. "We don't have much time. Brother Chris, these are my Brothers Harold, Lloyd, Vester, and Bob. Brothers, this is my Brother Chris from San Antonio."

We shook hands all around, and Bob said, "So this is who you tell all them stories to, and everyone thinks you are so durn smart and such. Brother Chris, you and I need to talk sometime."

"We don't have time for that," John interrupted as I nodded in agreement with Bob. "Let's get to it. Brother Harold, you see that the door is properly tiled."

Brother Harold replied, "Yes, Worsh.... I mean OK, John." He put a chair in front of the door and sat down.

While I stood there with my mouth hanging open in shock, the big box was opened, a big plastic bag was untied, and I watched as more food was pulled out than I thought could fit in that box. No wonder it took two Brothers to carry it. There was a chicken of every kind and description. There was fried chicken, baked chicken, chicken tenders, and even gizzards and livers, which I can do without, but the rest seemed to like them a lot. Next came out a pot of chicken and dumplings which made my mouth water uncontrollably. They then hauled out about ten ears of corn on the cob and a bowl of fried okra. I reached out for that right away before John could get his hands on it. Heck, they even had two loaves of homemade bread. I remarked that the only thing missing was something to wash it all down. That comment got me a sideways glance and a shake of the head by Brother Vester as he pulled out a gallon of tea, a gallon of lemonade, and cups for everyone.

We were all digging in when John seemed to remember something, turned, and called out across the room, "Mr. Jackson? Are you awake over there?" At that moment, I realized that this was a two-patient room and a long curtain separated the two beds.

"*Hell yes, I am awake,*" Mr. Jackson growled from the other side of the curtain. "How could anybody sleep with all that racket going on over there?"

"Well, I am sorry about that," John replied apologetically. "Are you hungry?"

"It's about time," Mr. Jackson growled again. "I thought you'd never ask. I was just about to push my panic button and have Nurse Mona break up your party. But you just bought my silence. Now pull this darn curtain out of the way and let me have some real food. I have been in here four days, and I can't take it anymore either."

We all ate fast and in total silence savoring all the wonderful tasting homemade food. The only family business discussed throughout the meal was that everyone needed to go to dinner at Brother Lloyd's house some night because his wife had made most of this feast.

Dear Reader,

It was a meal that I would drive five hours to have any time.

While the Brothers were cleaning up the mess we made, Brother Harold opened the window to let the smell dissipate.

Mr. Jackson broke the silence by saying, "You know that it's not going to take Nurse Mona long to figure out your little game."

"Whatever do you mean, Mr. Jackson," John asked with an innocent look on his face.

"I am just saying that she will figure out that you all are Masonic Brothers at some point, and she won't be happy. She is a by the book type of person."

"How did you figure out that we are Masons?" John asked.

"It really wasn't that hard," Mr. Jackson replied. "My father was a Mason. Anyway, thanks for dinner. Now pull that curtain and let me sleep."

John's food posse said their goodbyes and told John they would check on him after his surgery and left. I looked up at the clock, and it was already close to seven o'clock. I had to drive back that same night, so I needed to extract wisdom of any kind worth using in my column in less than an hour. I sure didn't want to be here when Mona came back.

In a low voice nodding towards the curtain that separated John's bed with Mr. Jackson's, "Do you have anything you want me to tell the Brothers who read the Newsletter?"

John pondered a moment before replying, "Don't worry about talking low. What I have to say can be said in front of anyone."

A low growl came from the other side of the curtain, "I would just as soon you keep it low. I'm trying to sleep."

John lowered his voice to just above a whisper, "Brother Chris, when did you decide to become a Mason?"

Oh my gosh, I thought to myself. *I am waiting to hear something profound and important, and John is asking personal questions.*

"I was initiated in 1984, John, so it must have been sometime before that. But what does that have to do with anything?"

"No, when did you decide to *become* a Mason?"

"Come on, John, what do you want me to say? I was raised to the Sublime Degree of a Master Mason in 1985. I guess I became a Mason then, right?"

"No, my Brother, you are not getting what I am asking," John said as he frowned at me.

"Then I am confused, John. You need to unconfuse me."

"Me too," chimed in the voice beyond the curtain. John and I looked at each other and then at the curtain.

"Brother Chris, people are always asking me when I became a Mason. I have always answered as you did. But the other day it hit me like a lightning bolt right between the eyes." John gave this dramatic demonstration of his idea of a lightning bolt hitting him right between the eyes.

"John, you need not be so dramatic and get to the point. Nurse Mona will be here any minute to kick me out."

"He's right," echoed Mr. Jackson from next door. "And you are giving me a headache. Get to it, man."

"*OK, OK, here it is,*" John said with an exasperated tone, glancing at the curtain as he spoke. "When you were initiated, you were made a Mason. When you were raised to the Sublime Degree of a Master Mason, you were told that you were entitled to all the *rights and benefits* of a Master Mason. Nowhere in your degrees, or your memory work, did anyone tell you, or did you read, that you had *become a Mason*. You know why? Because you hadn't.

Just because a man is initiated, passed, and raised does not mean he has *become a Mason*. Finishing the Degrees does not mean that instantaneously a Brother has *become* the man that our principles and teachings can mold him into becoming. Many, many, Brothers out there never decided to *become* a Mason. Sure, they had to be good men of good character even to be considered for membership into our gentle Brotherhood. But *becoming* a Mason takes time, study, reflection, and lots of hard work. It is no wonder that Masonry is a *Way of Life* because, for most Brothers, it becomes your life and is a lifetime work in progress. Given the proper amount of time and thought, it becomes a part of everything you say and do, every decision you make, and every life you touch. It inspires you to do things you never thought you could do. But just because you carry a membership card doesn't.... and I repeat, it doesn't mean you have *become a Mason*."

"I think I understand what you are saying, John. It is pretty easy to spot each of those Brothers who have *become* a Mason. There aren't that many of them."

"Yup, Brother Chris, but there are many, many, more Brothers out there who have made the conscious decision to begin the work necessary to become a Mason. All Masons are good men, but some don't know that they have already become everything Masonry is about. They have not an unkind word or thought, but always a thoughtful smile and a warm handshake. A Brother who you know immediately would do anything for you and who you could trust with your life. They are men who go about their lives doing good things for others without fanfare or recognition. Too many Brothers walk around with a membership card in their wallets and think that means they have become a Mason, but I can tell you that they are wrong in their thinking. There is a difference between being a good man and *becoming a Mason*. Now, do you know what I am talking about?"

Before I could answer, a sad-sounding voice from the other side of the curtain said, "Well, I sure do. You make an excellent point. I happen to be one of those card-carrying Brothers. I never made that decision to *become* a Mason."

John and I just stared at each other, not saying anything. I could imagine Mr...., apparently, Brother Jackson lying there staring at the ceiling absorbing John's words.

John finally broke the silence, "Why didn't you say you were a Mason before?"

I heard the Brother take a deep breath and blow it out, and then he said, "Well, I guess I was a little ashamed. Not ashamed to be a Mason but ashamed that I never learned how to be a true Mason. My Lodge Brothers were all good men, I am sure. But I never felt like I was one of them, and it was easier to not go to Lodge than to make a place for myself there. I figured that I was a Master Mason, so I was as much a Mason as any of them. But just now, I sadly realize that I never was." Then I heard Brother Jackson chuckle, "Brothers, I stopped believing in coincidences long ago. I believe that somehow, I was supposed to be right here tonight to hear what you said. Thank you for saying it, and thanks again for dinner. Now be quiet and let me sleep."

John and I just stared at each other with a dumb look on our faces. "So, Brother Chris, did I give you something to pass on to the Brothers?"

All I could do is shake my head and smile. "John, you surely did, and I will tell you what I think. I think you *became a Mason* a long time ago."

"I am not so sure about that, Brother Chris. But I appreciate you for saying it. I hope that when the Supreme Architect calls me home, he won't be disappointed in me."

All of a sudden, the door burst open, and there she was, Nurse Mona, and she had one of those HA, I caught you looks on her face. She looked around the room and seemed disappointed that the other Brothers were already gone, and then her eyes settled on me. I glanced at the clock and realized I was on her time. I could feel my hair prickling on the back of my neck as I stammered in a weak voice, "I was just leaving."

"You sure are; it's eight o'clock. Say your good-byes and get out. I'll be waiting outside," she growled.

Well, I just stood there frozen for a few seconds. I realized that my knees were shaking. "Boy, she scares the crap out of me, I am sure glad I am not in here."

"Thanks a lot," John whined. "You'd go and leave a Brother behind knowing how she is?"

"I feel confident that you and Brother Jackson can take her no problem," I said, not really meaning it.

"Don't count on it," came the voice from behind the curtain.

I realized that I needed to get while the getting was good. "OK, John, I gotta go now. I am glad that you are OK, and i'll check in with you after the surgery Brother."

"Here, take this box with you," John said quickly.

"No, John, what if she smells it. She will surely kick my rear end all over the place."

"Better you than me, besides I'm the one stuck with her. Now go!"

I grabbed the box and did what my Dad told me a long time ago to do in a tight situation. I kept a stiff upper lip, puckered my rear, and stepped out into the hall. Oh yes, she was waiting for me, all right. I said a little prayer to myself and ended with a whispered, "So Mote It Be." I prayed that I could get by Nurse Mona with this big box of food trash with my hide still intact. I boldly started for the elevator.

Then out of nowhere, something devious popped into my mind, and I thought, *what the heck*—changing my course to pass close by where she was standing with her hands on her hips and her eyes shooting daggers at me. As I went past her, I leaned in and whispered in her ear that John had told me that he thought she was a real hot chick. Boy! Nurse Mona reacted as if she had been slapped. As I got on the elevator, she was still standing in the same spot with a stunned look on her face.

I must have laughed half the way home. I made a mental note to myself not to answer any call from John for a couple of weeks. He was going to need time to cool off. I can't wait to see him next month.

IT'S HOW WE PRAY AND LEFT-OVER SURPRISE

The day started out well. Before the lunch hour, I got a call from a guy with the absolute worst Russian accent I have ever heard. He wanted to know about some work on his truck...heh heh.... yeah right. I just knew it was John. I wasn't rude to him, but I was intentionally vague. At one point, I asked what part of Russia he came from, and he kind of chuckled as I said it. The caller said he was from the Republic of Georgia. I asked if everyone from Georgia talked like him. He seemed a little puzzled by my questions, and I could sense he was getting a little irritated with my attitude, and of course, I was doing it on purpose. The caller asked me another question, and I started to give him another dig about his accent when I happened to glance up and .... *Ohhhhhh Crap!!!!* John Deacon was walking in the door.... and he wasn't on the phone. *Man, oh, man!!!* I started stuttering, stammering, and apologizing to my customer.

The more I tried to explain that I had been mistaken, the more confused and frustrated he got. After about 10 minutes of trying to make him understand that I wasn't making fun of him, he finally agreed to bring his truck in. I wanted to get off the phone as quickly as possible. John talked to Roger while I was eating a rather large helping of crow. I was sure it was John on the phone, which had gotten me into deep kimchi with my customer.

"Brother Chris, I think you need to work on your customer service skills because from where I'm standing, I don't think you did a good job communicating with the customer."

Yes, you are right; if you think I wanted to strangle him right then. But I know I need to take a step back and recover from this predicament. Instead, I decided to get out of the shop for a while. "Brother John, let's go get some lunch. And you are buying, period."

I stomped out the door with John, following with a confused look on his face. We took my truck because I needed to stop by my house and pick up some papers I had left there. John whined and moaned the whole way about how hungry he was. Except for his complaining, he didn't say much while driving, which was not the normal John.

John followed me into the house to have a glass of water while I searched for my papers. After a few minutes, I finally found what I was looking for. As I walked back towards the kitchen, I could see my big hound dog Nicki staring at something in the kitchen, and I swear there was a look of disbelief on her face. When I rounded the corner and walked into the kitchen, I saw that the whole kitchen table was covered entirely with containers of leftovers. John had his head inside my fridge, and all I could see was his rather sizable rear end staring at me. He jumped and bumped his head on one of the shelves when I yelled, *"John, what the heck are you doing?"*

John turned around with a startled look on his face. I saw the fried chicken leg hanging out of his mouth and two more containers in hand. He walked over to the table and sat the food containers down. Finally, he pulled the leg out of his mouth, "Brother Chris, you've got a lot, and I mean a lot of good stuff in there. Let's just eat here."

Ok Readers,

I need to explain some things here, so you don't get the wrong idea about my fridge. Pam and I work a lot of hours, and then I attend Lodge activities during the week, so we tend to eat out a few times a week. Most of the time, we end up with several take-out containers sharing space (most of the space actually) with the milk, juice, mayo, jelly, and everything else.

"Oh my gosh, I can't believe you have this in here! This right here is sooo good. Oh my, look at this. I love this stuff too!" Then John stopped all of a sudden and slowly pulled out an empty wrapper that had contained …. something …. and he looked at me and down at the empty wrapper and with a straight face said, "Brother Chris, I think something ate something else."

We just stood there looking at each other and that empty wrapper. John started to chuckle, and I couldn't help but join in. I finally had to snatch the empty wrapper out of his hands and throw it away. He immediately went back to removing more stuff. When John finally sat down at the table, there was no place to put our drink glasses. I just sat there in total awe as he first opened a container and smelled it. Apparently, it took a couple of seconds for the information from his nose to travel to his brain then back down to his mouth. Seconds later, the entire contents of the container were gone. He got up to heat up the leftover chicken alfredo and chicken fried steak in the microwave while he finished off a cucumber salad that Pam had left in there from the night before. Boy, she was not going to be happy about that. Nicki just sat there watching John with drool flowing out of the corners of her mouth. Still hungry, John opened up a container of beef and chicken fajitas. He walked back over to the fridge, found a few tortillas wrapped in foil, and then headed to the microwave to heat them up. I moved the trashcan closer to the table to make it easier to throw away empty wrappers and containers. I stacked up the plastic containers behind me so that I could wash them later. Little by little, I could see the top of the table again.

I looked over at Nicki, and her eyes were fixated on John. She was patiently waiting for him to drop something, but she didn't know John like I did. Nothing was going to be dropped. I glanced over as he opened a plastic bowl, and I saw several leftover pork chops. I reached across to grab one and nearly lost a couple of fingers. John growled and snapped at me like a dog. If I don't want to lose any appendages, I should go check out the fridge. I opened the fridge to see if I could snatch something that he had missed, but all I found was a carton of orange juice and a bottle of mustard. He had totally cleaned it out. Frustrated, I went back and sat at the table. After a few minutes of my glaring at him, John grudgingly slid a couple of BBQ Brisket chunks and one scraggly pork chop my way.

I could see that he was slowing down a bit and finally when there was nothing else, John let out a big sigh. "Brother Chris, we need to eat here more often. That was awful good, and it is quiet because nobody is bothering us."

"Yeah, right. You are full, and I'm still hungry. If you have got anything to talk about this month, you better get to it because I have to get back to work."

"I am in distress. Something happened last week that really bothered me, and I guess I need to vent. But first, I need to wash my hands."

While he was distracted, I rummaged through the pantry and found a box of old-fashioned oatmeal and raisin cookies. I was sitting at the table guarding my food while I ate when he got back.

"Brother Chris, are you eating dessert behind my back?"

"No, John. This is the only food left in the house, and I don't feel like sharing. I am not trying to be mean, but I have to eat something if I am going to be able to survive the rest of the day at work."

John just stood there glaring at me until I handed over the box. There was a handful left, but I knew that he was going to finish them off.

"I noticed that you were quieter than usual today. Are you OK, John?"

"No, I am not. I am in a little distress, and I really need to vent to someone. Don't you remember me saying that before you tried to eat all the cookies?"

"You go ahead and be the venter, and I will be your vente." I was trying to joke with him, but John was not in a joking mood. He sat there looking out the window for a few seconds before speaking. He started talking slowly with a voice so low that I had to lean towards him slightly to hear him.

"I was visiting a different Lodge the other night. The Chaplain concluded the prayer by saying 'in the name of Jesus' instead of in the name of God or the Supreme Architect of the Universe. What was worse is that I was the only one in the Lodge that seemed to be concerned about it."

"You are kidding me. What did you do?"

"Well, after the meal and before we went into Lodge, I took the Chaplain aside to speak to him. I have known him forever, but he was upset when I asked him why he did it. His response was, 'Well, Brother John, I am a Christian, and that's the way Christians pray.' I told him that he couldn't do that in a Masonic Lodge, and he got confrontational. He said if they don't like it, they could kick him out of Masonry.

Brother Chris, when he said that somethin' inside me just snapped. I was so upset that I told him, 'Then let me have your dues card, and you can leave.' The Brother just stood there and looked at me with a dazed look on his face. After a short pause, he asked if I was serious because I should know him well enough to know that Masonry is his life.

I shook my head, collected my thoughts before I responded to him. 'I do realize that, but it seems that you have lost your way, or you just don't get it. You do realize that what you did not only is against the Grand Lodge Law of every Grand Lodge in this country, but it also violates one of the most basic tenets of Masonry?' His response was, 'all the Brothers in this Lodge are Christians anyway, so I don't see what the big deal is.'

At this point, I noticed a few Brothers had gathered around us and were listening to the conversation. I started feeling a little uncomfortable, but I had to push on. 'I just want to ask you something Brother Chaplain. What if there was a Brother in the room right then who was not a Christian? Being your Brother, he may not have been offended by what you did but the fact is that you just left him out of the prayer. Brothers do not ever leave their Brothers out.'

The Chaplin just looked at me with a hurt look on his face, and then without saying a word, he turned and walked into the Lodge. I felt terrible right then, and I had surely upset the Lodge's peace and harmony but gol darnit, he was wrong, and somebody needed to say it. We all went into Lodge. When it was time for the Chaplain to read the standard prayer opening, he did so without mentioning any God, then he paused for a couple of seconds and said, 'Amen.' I met his eyes across the Lodge Room and just shook my head. I could see he was deep in thought, but he still didn't get it.

So, at the appropriate time, I stood up and addressed the WM and the Wardens by saying, 'Brethren, Masonry treats every man the same regardless of his age, race, financial level, class, political views, or his religious affiliation. In Masonry, no man is better or worse than another. It follows then that Masonry regards no religion as better or worse than another. Praying to God or the Supreme Architect of the Universe and not to your God specifically is not intended to, nor does it lower the importance or significance of your faith. It shows that just as all Masons meet upon the level, so are all faiths equal and welcome within Masonry. Masonry doesn't care what your chosen faith is. It only cares that a Mason believes in God, and you all know that. You may call your God anything you wish. That's why Masonry works, my Brothers. I assure you there are men out there, good men, and maybe also good Brothers who are not of the same faith as you who, if they chose to or if they have wanted to come to Lodge or maybe wanted to join Masonry, would change their minds because of the prayer that was offered here tonight.'

I thanked the WM for allowing me to speak and sat down. Before he could say anything, the Chaplain slowly stood, and after being recognized, he apologized to the Lodge for forgetting how to be a Mason. He followed that up by thanking me for turning on the light again.

When he sat down, a Brother who overheard our conversation outside the door rose to his feet. You could tell that he was having trouble coming up with the right words to express himself. He said that even though he was not of the same faith as all the Brothers in the Lodge, he loved the Lodge and his Brothers just the same. Though he never was offended by the previous prayers, he felt like he was excluded from them. He thanked the Chaplain for being a good Brother. A couple of other Brothers stood and thanked the Chaplain for doing the right thing. It all turned out OK in the end, so I am glad I said something."

"Oh, wow, John. What a great story. So, what are you down in the dumps about? To me, it seems like everything got resolved."

"I just can't help thinking that there are more Lodges and more of our Brothers out there who have lost their way also."

"You don't think they are doing it to purposely hurt the Fraternity, do you?"

"I do think it is on purpose but not to hurt Masonry. I think that the Brothers who do this don't fully understand what they are doing. They haven't thought about the damage it can and will do to their Lodge, the Fraternity, and to themselves as Masons. I really think it goes back to Masonic education or the lack of it. There are so many Brothers out there who don't have a clue about what Masonry stands for. But it's not because they don't want to know. It's that our Lodges have become supper clubs instead of learning institutions like they were meant to be. It's nobody's fault but our own."

"But John, there are only 10% to 15% of all the Brothers that are Masons that come to Lodge. How are you going to teach all of them?"

"The reality is that we are never going to teach all Brothers, but the ones that come to Lodge can and need to get a steady diet of Masonic education. And it can be done at every Stated Meeting in a way that is not only informative but interesting and entertaining. I know this is true because we are doing it at our Lodge, and it is working well. I know the Brothers want to learn the lessons in Masonry. We just have to provide those lessons. If we do this, many of our absent Brothers will come back to Lodge. We also have to make them understand that Masonry is not about just one thing. The basic tenets of Freemasonry: free-thinking, freedom of expression, freedom to worship how you choose, and the bond of Brotherly love are all elements of the whole of Freemasonry. It's like that glue. You know that glue, right?"

"Glue? Good Lord John, I hate it when you go off on all these analogies. What the heck are you talking about?"

He fixed me with a hard stare while he was thinking, and then the light came back on. "Epoxy... that's the glue. It's like Epoxy. You know how Epoxy has two or more ingredients that you have to mix together to make the glue stick? Each ingredient by itself won't glue anything together. But when all the ingredients are put together, they will hold together and never break apart. Masonry, my confused Brother is a lot like that."

"Ok, John, I get it. I agree with you. Do you feel better now that you got all that off your chest?"

"Awww, not really. I needed to say it to someone, but the problem isn't getting any better. Something needs to be done, and it falls to all of us to do it. We can't wait for someone else to do it."

"I really do agree, John. I've got to get back to work. I need to earn some money to buy more food. So, load it up."

John didn't say much on the trip back to the shop. He just sat there staring out of the window. If I had eaten what he ate, I wouldn't have been able to talk, walk, or anything else, but that wasn't his problem. He just had a lot on his mind, I suspect.

Just as I drove into the parking lot at the shop, "Brother Chris, I am thankful that I have you to talk to about all these things. When I have something, I need to say you are always there to listen. I thank you for that."

I just smiled and nodded. "Brother John, it does me as much good as it does you. I really enjoy talking to you too."

MASONIC HYPOCRISY AND THE SUPER SONIC

I was driving down the freeway heading towards town with a plastic gas can full of diesel in the back of the truck. No, I didn't need the extra gas. My truck doesn't run on diesel. I was on the way to rescue Brother John, who had run out of gas on his way to have our monthly lunch. I gave him as much grief about not watching the gauge as I could over the phone and then headed out on the rescue mission. Neither he nor the truck was hard to spot. I pulled up behind him and got out to retrieve the gas can. I waited for him to dismount Ol' Blackie as I put the fuel in the tank, but he never got out. To be honest, that irritated me a bit. I finished putting in the fuel, and as I was on my way to jerk open his door to drag him out of the truck when I heard a voice calling my name. It kinda sounded like John, but it wasn't coming from the truck. I looked around, and you are not going to believe what I saw; Brother John across the street sitting at an aluminum table under a canopy at a Sonic Drive-In.

"Are you just going to stand there?" he yelled over the noise of traffic going by. "Come on over and eat with me. I'm buying."

That was two unbelievable things: John at a Sonic and offering to buy me lunch. This was indeed a strange day. Actually, I was thinking about making up somewhere that we ate instead of reporting to you that we ate at a fast-food drive-in. I am sure your opinion of John has dropped a couple of notches, but it is what it is. There he sat in all his rotundness, finishing up something that looked like a double-decker burger.

"What a big surprise," I said, a little out of breath after dodging all the cars trying to get across the busy street. "I am a little shocked at finding you here."

"I got hungry while I was waiting for you to get here. I couldn't help it, and heck, the food is pretty good here. And to top it off, they are playing all the songs I like."

"Are you kidding me? Sixties rock and roll is your kind of music? What about George Strait?"

"Brother Chris, I happen to be a connoisseur of many things and music is one of them. George Strait is right up there with Brother John Wayne."

"You know that John Wayne was not a singer, don't you?"

"Don't confuse the issue. I like the food and the music here, and that is that. Now sit yourself down. I'll show you what else is good here."

As I sat down, he twisted around in his chair and pressed the big red button on the menu. Immediately a young female voice came over the speaker and said, "Yes sir, Mr. John. What can I get you now?"

"Well, the surprises just keep on coming. They already know you by name here? That didn't take long. Just how many times have you pushed this button John?"

He frowned and motioned me to be quiet while he ordered himself another double jalapeno burger with cheese, a big order of tater tots, and a large chocolate shake. As an afterthought, he added two corn dogs and a foot-long chili dog. Heck, my stomach was starting to get a little queasy thinking about all of the food. I actually thought he might be ordering for me too until he turned and motioned for me to tell the box what I wanted. After I finished, he slid his credit card through the reader mounted just below the voice box.

"So, what do you mean by you'll show me what is good here? I doubt you plan on sharing any of the food you just ordered with me."

"No, that's not what I was talking about." His eyes were watching the front door as he spoke. "Just wait. It will be happening in just a minute."

As if on cue, the door burst open. Two teenage girls on roller skates were heading in our direction at a high-speed jostling position, which I thought was weird considering they were carrying our lunch. I was starting to worry that they wouldn't stop, but I found out quickly that they had no intention of stopping as they roared by us, skated around our table and headed back the way they came. I was having flashbacks of the '70s and the Bay Area Bombers of the California Roller Derby. They had turned back towards us, giggling and pushing and shoving and skated right up to us before sliding to a stop all out of breath. I looked over at John who was laughing his head off. He gave the girls the thumbs-up as they placed our well-traveled meal in front of us. Then they zipped off back to the kitchen as fast as they could skate, hip checking and elbowing all the way.

"Wasn't that great? Last time the other one got here first."

I just sat there without expression as John dug right in and motioned for me to do the same. Heck, I was out of breath, and I was just sitting there. Finally, I got my breathing under control and began to eat. I knew the conversation was over for the most part until he was finished eating. Before I finished my lunch, he ordered himself two corn dogs. Unbelievably both waitresses, each with one corn dog only on the tray, traveled around our table again at a high rate of speed. They were giving and taking shots you usually only see in a boxing ring. They dropped John's corn dogs on the table as they flew by and raced back to the kitchen. I wondered where they got all that energy.

"John, don't order anything else. I don't think I can take another lap around our table."

He grinned and attacked his corn dogs, devouring both in no time flat. He sat back with a contented look on his face. "Yup, lunch and entertainment. This was a very good lunch."

"I would never have thought you would be caught dead dining here. I hope you have some serious profundity to offer the Brothers this month. As it is, I am going to have to make up something about where we had lunch."

"As a matter of fact, I have something to say if you like pain, discomfort, and sadness."

"I don't know if I want to hear how you feel after you eat a meal." That got me a John Belushi, one eyebrow raised, stern stare.

"That's not what I mean, and you know it. I want to tell you a really sad story. You know, I was thinking on the way down here about a Brother who just affiliated with our Lodge. He's a real good guy. I talked to him the other day, and I asked him why he was affiliated with our Lodge. He got kind of a sad look on his face. I could tell he wasn't very comfortable talking about it, but finally, he said to me that he just got tired of all the same old thing. That got me to wonder about the feller a little bit if he was one of those who wanted to change the ritual and do away with the memory work and all. I was starting to wish I hadn't asked, and he must have sensed it because he continued on to tell me that he had been a Brother for nearly 20 years and was a Past Master of his Lodge. He said that his Lodge was dying. That there were 4 or 5 Brothers .... all Past Masters that literally ran the Lodge and wouldn't allow anyone to do anything new. He felt that with their actions, these Brothers had intimidated the younger members. The new Brothers refused to even serve as officers anymore, and other younger members left the Lodge completely. He told me that no one could agree on anything, and because of that, no one even tried anymore. That story brought back many sad memories from what I have seen over the years. I sure do hate thinking about this stuff, but like I heard a guy say on TV the other day, 'It is what it is.' So now I'm all riled up about it, and I have to say what I have to say."

I knew there no use trying to stop him, and I wasn't sure I really wanted to. My biggest fear was that John would get so enthusiastic that it would be difficult to get him to keep his voice down, but I would try my best. He was almost in high gear by now, and the emotion was pouring out simultaneously.

"It's about pride Brother Chris. We have to regain our pride in the Fraternity somehow. I think we, and I am talking about the Craft, have transitioned into what we are today little by little, losing our identity over time. I hear coaches and managers of sports teams when they are interviewed after losing a game that they should have won saying, 'we just stopped doing the things we do well. We went away from the game plan, and we stopped being who we are.' When I hear that, I know that's what happened to us too. We stopped being proud to be Masons. We started making excuses for who we are and what we do. Then we started trying to change the Craft to fit some ridiculous model of what would make people not say bad things about us. We try to attract new Brothers in the organization who otherwise would not or could not join. We ran, Brother

Chris. We retreated with our tails between our legs instead of holding our heads high and being who we are and what we are supposed to be. We are the ones who should be changing. Masonry is the good and the right. It should be the guiding light for what is good and what is right in the world. Why would we back away from those who would attack us? After all, it is because of their own ignorance that they think we are something we aren't. The result is that we have lost our identity. People don't have a clue who and what we really are anymore. Is it any wonder that we are losing members? We just don't matter anymore.

We have become irrelevant. I see our lack of pride in the condition of our Lodge buildings and properties. I see it in the way our Brothers dress for Lodge functions. I see it in the attendance at our meetings. I see it in the lack of respect for the work when we can't open or close a Lodge correctly or perform a Degree the right way. We have lowered our standards throughout the Fraternity to the point that we regularly let in men who are not properly investigated, and we find out too late that they are not the kind of men we want in Masonry. Is it any wonder that our pride in the Craft is all but gone when we allow men to become Masons whose motivations are other than Masonic in nature? The result of this is that men who are of the type of character the Craft needs and wants choose not to seek membership. It's obvious to them that we'll take just anybody. Our exclusive membership becomes just any old Tom, Dick, or Harry, and prospective members can see that.

We have Brothers, and I use the term loosely, saying that they have no ulterior motives and aggressively use the Craft and their Brothers to promote their businesses and their social status. It's the ultimate hypocrisy when you say that you only allow a certain type of man for membership and then accept without question those who don't meet your own minimum standards. And the reason these Masonic wannabe's get in is because we don't have enough pride. I repeat pride. Enough to follow our own rules when investigating potential candidates. It's what our Grand Master calls 'being asleep at our West Gate,' and boy is he right on the money. And if that's not enough, we have all but stopped dispensing Masonic Education in the Lodges. Many Brothers don't even know what Masonry really is. They didn't receive a Masonic education, history, or discussion at all. Just eat, shoot the breeze, and whine and moan about why no one comes to Lodge anymore. Open and close the Lodge poorly and go home. That's all it is to many of our Brothers."

Now his face was beet red. I could see the veins sticking out on his face and head. I was wondering when he would take a breath. Heck, I was also hoping he wouldn't have a heart attack. The people in a few of the closest cars had shocked looks on their faces. I could tell that they didn't really understand what was going on, except that the big guy was not happy.

"We have way too many Lodges that are just plain mismanaged. They don't even deserve to have a Charter. They disgrace the Fraternity, and it appears that they just don't care. I hear Brothers all the time saying that their Lodge can't afford to take care of their buildings. I say bull corn to that!! They just need to take some pride and get off their lazy keesters and get it done. There are only about a million different ways to raise money. But a fundraiser of any kind takes energy and a desire to get it done. And oh yes, ... it takes pride! We need to quit swapping dollars with other Masons and do some fundraisers that attract the general public. We would actually address two issues that way. We would make more money for Lodge, and at the same time, would raise our profile in the community. Why don't we see these things? And not being able to learn to open and close a Lodge .... give me a break, will ya. I could take most any person off the street and have them opening and closing a Lodge in less than a couple of hours ..... perfectly. Like my Daddy used to tell me, 'Don't pee on my leg and tell me it's raining.' I just ain't buying it."

His voice was way too high and too loud. I don't think he even noticed I gave him the universal calm down signal by raising and lowering my arms. I thought about using the Grand Hailing Sign to get his attention, but I was not in actual distress. I was actually agreeing with everything he was saying. How could I not? After all, he was right. He had tears streaking down both cheeks.

"Why can't we see what we have become, Brother Chris? We've got to get our pride back before it's too late. Until we get our pride back, things will not get better. I don't know what it will take. Maybe it will take some Lodges going out of business before everyone gets the picture. Something needs to be done before we become just a men's social supper club. We need leaders. We need men who care, men who have courage. We need men who have a sense of right and a burning desire to do it right. Where are those men, Brother Chris? Do you know where we can find those men?"

All I could do is stare at him. I had no answers.

"Do you want me to tell you where those men are?"

I was still in shock, so I gave him a little nod. I thought I could see the smoke coming out of his ears.

"Those men are already in our Lodges. That's where they are. They are being smothered by Brethren, who don't even realize that they are destroying their Lodges. We've all heard it before, haven't we? You can't do that. That's not the way we've always done it in this Lodge. You can't do that because it won't work. When they say that, it's laziness talking. Yup, it's a lack of pride. I heard about a Lodge that hadn't updated their law book since 1989. When asked why they said that it was because they liked the Law Book that year. When I heard that my head dang near fell off. Brother Chris, there are leaders out there. Now mind you, we don't need bosses or dictators. We need good and true leaders! I'm telling you from experience, there's a big difference. We need these leaders to stop taking no for an answer, step up, lead their Brothers and their Lodges, and bring back the pride. And when they do, they will bring back Masonry."

As he reached into his pocket for his handkerchief to wipe his eyes, a horn honked. We both turned and saw a man giving John the thumbs up, which we returned. I wondered how what John had said pertained to him, but as he drove away, I saw the Masonic license plate on his truck, and then I knew.

"Brother John. You get me so pumped up sometimes I want to give you a big hug."

"Whoa there, my Brother," he said as he threw his arms up in front of himself defensively with a big grin on his face. "You need to subdue your passions and get a hold of yourself."

"Come on, John. You know that's not what that means. Cut it out."

He smiled now that he had expressed all of his frustrations for the day. "Are you going to buy me some dessert?"

"Come on, John, you still owe me for the fuel I brought. In fact, I have contributed so much support this year that I am considering putting you on my taxes as a dependent."

"So, this is the thanks I get after I paid for lunch and the entertainment? I guess I'll just have to pay for dessert, and we'll just call 'err even."

Before I could respond, he pushed the magic red button, ordered two big banana splits, and swiped the card. Then he sat back and waited. I noticed several cars had pulled in, and the occupants were enjoying their corn dogs and their tater tots. My only thought as the kitchen door flew open was I sure hoped they all liked Roller Derby.

THE VI-BER-ATOR AND THE DREAM

I got the call at about 11:30 last Thursday, and John interrupted me as soon as he heard my voice.

"I already know where you are taking me to eat."

"And how are you doing today, Brother John? Please enlighten me as to where we are going so I can call my banker and get a loan to pay for it."

"You do realize that's not funny. But no matter. You need to meet me at Olive Garden because I saw a TV commercial the other day about all you can eat soup, salad, and breadsticks."

Uh oh, big red flag. "John, I don't know if that is a really good idea. Don't you remember we almost got thrown out of the last place that had all you can eat? I don't want to go through that again."

"Don't you worry yourself about it, Brother Chris. I plan on ordering a bunch of other stuff so they won't get upset."

Wow, I thought, shaking my head in disbelief. I have never known someone who could solve a problem and create a whole new one at precisely the same instant, but John sure could. I wondered if it was his duty in life to run me into bankruptcy. I decided to just go with it, hoping we could have lunch without him making a scene. I wanted to be able to eat there again since it was kinda close to my house. But alas, it was not to be. I told him to go ahead and get there and put our name on the list because it is almost always at-least a 30-minute wait. I only have an hour for lunch. I waited for about 20 minutes after we hung up before I started heading down there. When I got to the restaurant, I found him with his hands on his hips and a big scowl on his face. He was standing with a whole bunch of other people waiting for a table. I eased between a couple of ladies who seemed to be as unhappy as John was about waiting.

"Hello there, John. How much longer is the wait?" Standing next to him, I realized that his lower lip stuck out like a pouting 10-year-old kid.

"Brother Chris, nobody knows anything. They gave me this little contraption (a 6-inch square piece of plastic) and said it would start a flashin' and a viberating (yes he said vib-er-rating) when we could eat. I ain't never seen anything like this. I am hungry big time."

"The hostess ought to know how much longer we will be. I don't have all day. And I doubt they want to see how you get when you're hangry."

"You're darn right. No one wants to avoid that more than me. I'll see if I can find out for both our sakes."

I followed him to the hostess station where two attractive and pleasant young ladies were being badgered one by one by the whole room. John asked one of them how much longer we were going to be waiting around, and she told him it shouldn't be much longer. It was clear that John was still not understanding how the pager worked. Had I known what a big drama it was going to be beforehand, I would have kept my mouth shut, but I opened my mouth and asked the hostess if she had checked to see if it worked before she gave it to John.

She kind of cocked her head and gave me a serious look. Without saying a word, she punched a code onto her panel, setting off John's vi-ber-rator. That one action set off a chain reaction neither I nor anyone else could have predicted. As soon as that pager went off in John's hand, he let out a loud "*Here we go!*" Before anyone could stop him, John started for the dining room.

The hostess yelled, "*Sir.... Siiirrrr. You can't....!*" but John was already gone. She looked back at me with a glare that I could actually feel the heat. The hostess took off after John with me right on her heels. By the time we found John, he was already sitting at a table. A waitress by the name of Lynn was taking his, uhh... our drink order. The hostess marched right up to John and told him that his table was not ready yet and to come back to the front.

"Hold on there, little lady. My vi-ber-rator thingy went off, so it was our turn."

She turned around and glared at me again. All I could do was mouth the words "I'm sorry," which didn't seem to help her mood at all. As she turned to lay into John, a guy who apparently was one of the managers walked up and said to the hostess, "It's ok. I will take it from here."

After the hostess left, he turned back to John and me. "That was by far one of the smoothest scams I have ever seen, and if it hadn't been so funny, I would have let Ana have at you. I know you didn't plan it, but it was funny, just the same. Enjoy your meal."

I sat down and gave John the angriest look I could muster. He shrugged his shoulders, spread his hands out in front of him, and said in a weak voice, "But the thingy went off."

I refused to talk to him. Lynn came back with our drinks and we ordered our food. She must have wondered why we decided to have lunch together when we obviously had a problem being around one another. The whole ordeal didn't faze John's appetite. True to form, he ordered all-you-can-eat soup, salad, and breadsticks. Then he ordered the Steak Gorgonzola Alfredo, which is a meal and a half for most people. As usual, I had to call the waitress back because she thought he was ordering for me too. Out of the corner of my eye, I noticed an older couple glaring at us from a couple of tables away and two ladies sitting to our left who were doing the same. I wondered why they were mad at us until I realized that we had probably been behind them in line for a table when John pulled his stunt. John noticed it too, because he was trying hard to keep from looking at them.

I decided to break my silence. "John, you know why they are mad at us, don't you?" He just stared at me, so I continued, "When your *thingy* went off, we got seated before them. And from the cold stares we are receiving I reckon that they were in front of us in line. If I'm being honest, I don't blame them for being upset with us."

"I never thought about that," he said apologetically. "I don't want them mad at me."

"Well, it's a little too late for that, Brother. You just have to accept that you are the bad guy right now."

"Don't worry, I will fix it. That was not what I intended to do, but I will make it right. Don't you worry Brother."

I didn't know how he would do it, but he needed to do something if he wanted to get back into their good graces. Our food finally came, and he kept finishing his soup and asking for more. I can't remember how many times she refilled the salad bowl or how many bowls of soup he consumed. I stopped counting at six. In between bowls of soup and salad, he managed to consume the entire Steak Gorgonzola plate. As John ate, he kept eyeballing my plate, just waiting for me to get distracted so that he could take it. I felt like I needed to curl my arm around my plate and guard it to keep him from taking it. It sure is hard to eat like that. I feel sorry for Mrs. Deacon. That poor lady has to deal with his habits daily and is probably tired of replenishing the refrigerator after every meal. If I were her, I'd make him pay for his own food to put in the refrigerator.

At one point, John was carrying on a low conversation with Lynn, no doubt ordering another of the four varieties of soup. I figured I would have to leave her a really good tip for the extra mileage she was putting in for John. Finally, he seemed to be getting to a stopping point, so I figured it was as good a time as any to see if he had any words of wisdom. I was hoping that he did. That way, I could take my mind off of what happened earlier.

"Brother Chris, there are profound lessons in most everything you see every day. I was at the Barber Shop the other day when an older man came in wanting to know how much a shampoo and a set would cost him. The Barber gave him a price and sat him down in the chair. When he took off his hat, the Barber said, 'But sir, you only have three hairs on your head.'

The old man said, 'I know. Just comb one to the right and one to the left and one straight back.'

So, the Barber started shampooing his hair. After just a few seconds, he said, 'Oops! One of your hairs just broke off, and you only have two left.'

The old man said, 'It's OK when you are done, just put one to the right and one to the left."

Dear Reader,

I have to tell you that I was really starting to wonder what the "profound lesson" was here. I decided to just wait it out and see where

John was going with today's conversation. We have had enough drama for one day, don't you think?

John saw the look on my face and shot me a narrow-eyed look and went on, "So the Barber resumed his shampooing, and a few seconds later he said once again, 'Oops. Sir, another one of your hairs just broke off. You only have one left. What do you want me to do?'

The old man thought for a few seconds and finally said, 'Oh heck, with it, just finish the shampoo and leave it messed up."

While I sat there with my mouth hanging open in confusion, John broke into a way too loud and way too long fit of laughter that sounded like a screeching hyena. After realizing that people were staring at us, he quieted down, wiping the tears out of his eyes.

"John, what was the lesson in that story? That is five minutes of my life that I can never get back."

"There isn't a lesson, at least not one that I know of. I liked the story, so I wanted to tell it. Don't you think it's a great story?"

Dear Reader,

I cannot repeat my exact words that came out of my mouth here. But basically, I told him to cut the comedy act and tell me something worth printing in the newsletter. I explained to him that there was no way I was going to put that story in there. (But I guess that wasn't exactly true).

John looked around like he was worried that someone might hear him. "Brother Chris, I had a dream the other night. I don't ever have dreams. Or if I do, I don't ever remember them. But the other night, I dreamed something that seemed so real. Heck, it just might have been real for all I know.

You know that I have been agitated about some of the things that are going on in Masonry. Things like the loss of members and our lackadaisical attitude towards preserving the purity and accuracy of the work, and the general lack of pride in our fraternity. I have been thinking about all of it for a while and quite frequently. I guess that is why I had the dream. I don't think I can ever forget it.

Anyway, it started at a Lodge. In my dream, I realized that I was in the anteroom being prepared to be initiated as an Entered Apprentice Mason. I remember feeling odd about it since I was already a Master Mason. I don't know why I didn't say anything or if I wasn't able to speak. It was almost like I was watching all that was going on from a few feet away. No one spoke, and soon I was at the door knocking for admission. When I was admitted, it was in total darkness. I strained to hear and understand every sound, every word spoken. I knelt, declared my fidelity to God, and then was led for what seemed to be the longest time through several passageways and doors with great commotion. All this happened with my companion, my friend, having to vouch for my character and ask that I be allowed to proceed. It struck me that I didn't even know him, yet he was pledging his honor that I was worthy of admission. After every obstacle was cleared, I could feel his firm grip on my arm, reassuring me that all was well.

We turned a corner, and I was given the last opportunity to back out. With nervous anticipation and a firm resolve, I asked to go on. I then knelt at the altar of Freemasonry and took an oath to God to be the man he wishes me to be. With my heart pounding with excitement from the profound lessons I had just learned, I was led to another place, and then another where

I received more lessons. Then I was back in the anteroom where I was astonished to find myself being prepared for another degree. While all this was going on, Brother Chris, it occurred to me that I was still in darkness. Needless to say, I was a little confused. I asked why I was still in darkness, but no answer was given. Words floated in and out of my memory 'that my mind might conceive before my eyes beheld.' I stopped worrying.

Soon, still in darkness, I found myself traveling again but in a different place, it seemed. Once again, I found myself kneeling and promising God to strengthen my mind and body and purifying my character to his satisfaction. I was told that to complete this part of my journey I would have to pass more tests and be vouched for again. I was also told that my ancient Brethren who desired further knowledge, traveled the same path. Even though I couldn't see, I was guided by the words spoken by my friend who now called me Brother. With his guidance, I could see the path before me. First, those sacred columns towered before me and then a stairway to an unknown place where I would find the answers I sought. Slowly and carefully, we climbed the winding steps, and even in darkness I could feel their pattern under my feet. Their lessons and meanings were passed from instructive tongue to my attentive ear.

My Brother held me close and guided me with confidence through the narrow passageways where we once again had to prove ourselves worthy in order to pass. Everything was familiar to me, yet my understanding was much more vivid. We passed the last test and found ourselves standing alone in what seemed to be a large room. I could hear the tiniest echo in my Brother's voice as he prepared me to receive further light.

My nervousness had returned as my Brother described our surroundings. I soon realized that we were not alone after all. The

Worshipful Master had been there all along. I had heard his voice and others during my travels, but none were Brothers that I knew. However, their voices seemed vaguely familiar somehow. This only added to my confusion. The Master then gave me the answers to the questions I had asked. Still in the darkness, I smiled as his words gave me light. I was then ordered to return whence I came, and preparation began for one more journey.

Brother Chris, I knew something big was coming in my subconscious, but I couldn't quite get a clear picture in my mind. Before I could figure it out, I was off again on another trek. This, by far, was the longest of the three. As we walked and climbed, we passed places where sacred words were being spoken. Some I could hear close by and others farther away, but we were never far from their comfort. Again, as before, new obstacles prevented us from continuing without certain assurances from my Conductor/Brother. Each time, he convinced the keepers of our sincerity and allowed us, sometimes grudgingly, to continue our journey.

Once again, we came to a place where I solemnly took my third obligation to God, my Country, my neighbor, and myself. After the prayer for my well-being, I stood to receive more of the light that I was promised. I found out to my surprise that I had another and an even more dangerous road to travel. I was to follow the footsteps of our ancient patron Hiram. Before I could react, all hell broke loose. My conductor pulled me along as if trying to escape the commotion. People were yelling at us. They wanted something from me, it seemed, but I did not have the answer. We fled from place to place, trying to get away, but there would be no escape.

Suddenly my life passed before my eyes. I felt my spirit being carried away as I silently asked the Great Architect of the Universe for strength and forgiveness. A cold and empty feeling came over me: all was lost, a sense of being alone. I felt that my journey was over and that somehow, I had failed. So many emotions were going through my mind. I was confused and honestly a little bit scared. I strained to hear what was going on. Everyone was looking for something, and I realized it was me, but somehow, they couldn't find me. I wanted to call out to them, but I couldn't. I could hear my Brothers praying for guidance and strength. Then they were trying to reach me. My heart was pounding in my chest as I willed them to succeed. All at once, a firm grip pulled me free and gave me a new life. I was overcome with happiness and relief as I held on tightly to my Brother. He gave me those last lessons that would last an eternity.

I heard the Worshipful Master give orders to my Brother/Conductor. He took my arm again to lead me to the East. Upon arriving there, my veil of darkness was lifted. Below a brightly lit letter "**G**" with a Masters jewel around his neck stood Brother George Washington. He smiled and nodded his head at me in acceptance. I just stood there with my mouth open in shock as he proceeded to welcome me and introduce the Brethren in the room. As my eyes followed him around the room, my disbelief was overwhelming.

Brother Ben Franklin nodded to me from the West, and Brother Sam Houston waved and smiled from the South. Brother Will Rogers was sitting in the Junior Deacons chair. That familiar voice I kept hearing in the anteroom belonged to Brother John Wayne, our Master of Ceremonies. Now I knew why he kept calling me 'Pilgrim.' As I circled the room, my eyes paused on every Brother. I recognized Jim Bowie, Anson Jones, and Stephen F. Austin. On the opposite side of the room Brothers Winston Churchill and Douglas McArthur sat together.

I struggled with the emotions of everything that had happened, but more importantly, I wondered why all of this happened. As I turned back to the East, I glanced over to finally see who had been my Friend/Brother/Conductor; David Crockett. He was the one who had brought me through all my journeys and made sure I arrived safely; now offering me a warm Brotherly grip.

I can tell you, Brother Chris, my knees were pretty weak and shaking by this time. It ws a miracle that I was still able to stand on my own. Then Brother George spoke to me, 'My Brother, I know that you have been troubled lately with all the problems that Masonry seems to have. I want to tell you and reassure you that Masonry has survived every kind of trial and calamity imaginable and still lives today. The Craft and her members have been persecuted, harassed, imprisoned, and even slaughtered over the many centuries. But she still lives on today. Her principles and teachings are perfect and pure and will withstand all tests. Masonry, my Brother, is like a soft and gentle breeze. Not something that you can see but always present and always residing in the hearts and minds of good and true men, giving strength and direction according to the will of the Supreme Architect of the Universe. Masonry, like the immortal soul of man, will never, never, never die. Each of these Brothers have heard you. They wanted to come to this place to remind you of the power and wonders within our gentle Craft's teachings. So that you may go forward to help reassure other Brethren that their labors are not in vain and that Masonry is and always will be a force for what is good and what is right. Do not despair, my Brother. Know that countless Brothers before you have struggled as you do. Because of those struggles, Masonry is as strong as ever no matter how few or how many the membership.'

Before I could thank him and the other Brothers he said, 'Go now and forever keep Masonry and your Brothers in your heart. Go now and continue to live by the teachings of our Great Fraternity until we meet again at the Celestial Lodge above.' And with those words, the whole scene faded out.

The next thing I remember is my wife shaking me awake. She was asking, 'Are you alright, John? You woke me up with all that talking in your sleep. You were saying *Thank you, Thank you,* and I looked over to see tears rolling down your cheeks.'

It took me a minute to get my head clear. I told her that I was ok, and to go back to sleep. It's been a few days, but now and again, she catches me deep in thought, replaying the dream in my head. From the looks she gives me, I think she is convinced I am losing my mind. Heck, she may be right. It was the most remarkable thing that has ever happened to me. I will never forget it. So that's it. Do you think I am crazy?"

"Crazy? Heck, John, I don't think you are crazy. I think you are the luckiest Brother I know. I got chills just listening to you. What a remarkable experience. Thank you for sharing."

I looked up, and the older couple we butted in front of were leaving, and they were headed straight for us. Here we go, I thought, we're going to get an earful from these guys. But to my total surprise, they walked up to John. The man stuck out his hand to shake John's, and the lady hugged him. They both said thanks to John and smiled at me as they walked away.

Lynn walked up and asked John if he wanted anything else. "Young lady, that last bite ruined my appetite. I think we are ready for the bill, and my Brother here is going to take care of it."

She looked at me and smiled as I handed her my credit card. When she returned, the two ladies who were mad at us had come over, and they too gave John, not me of course, hugs and thanked him. I was confused, but I decided that it wasn't worth asking. I'm used to being ignored when Big John is around.

John said he had to make a trip to the facilities and that he would wait for me outside. Lynn laid the charge slip down for me to sign. I apologized to her for all the trouble with John, and when I looked down at the charge slip, I nearly fainted. I knew it was going to be a lot because John eats as much as four people. I started taking inventory, and it seemed like I was paying for somebody else's lunch too. I waved Lynn over to show her there was a mistake on my bill. She smiled sweetly and told me that the gracious gentlemen sitting with me asked her to add the two other tables' meals to our tab. That's when it hit me. No wonder those other people were so lovely to him as they left. *I was paying for their lunches! That's how he planned to fix it.*

At this point, what could I do besides pay the bill? I signed the durn thing and made a beeline for the door, but more importantly, to find John. As I cleared the door, he roared past me in Ol' Blackie waving. I was waving too, but it wasn't exactly a friendly wave if you know what I mean.

I heard him yell out as he went by, "*Thanks for lunch, Brother Chris. I'll see you next month.*"

I continued to wave at him until an older lady walked by and gave me a dirty look. I will get even with him. You know what they say about paybacks.

A Masonic Rant and Raising the Flag

Dear Reader,

I was not looking forward to seeing my Brother John this month. In fact, after what he did to me last month, I kinda expected him to not come by this time. Heh, I should be so lucky. I had my head down working on the computer and didn't see him pull up to the shop. The whole front of the shop is all big windows, even the doors. Out of the corner of my eye, I noticed that something was blocking the sunlight. Hmmm, there has to be something symbolic in that. I looked up to see John standing outside the door, with a sheepish smile on his face waving at me. I seriously considered ignoring him, but he's real big, and heck, he is Brethren after all.

I waved him in with a frown; maybe he would take the hint that I was still upset about what happened. I still can't believe that he made it up to them by making me pay for their meals. He approached the desk with his head hanging low.

"I now appear before you in white gloves and apron and implore your pardon," the symbolism of which he knew I would understand.

I just gritted my teeth and counted to five, so I wouldn't say what was trying to force its way out of my mouth. Finally, I swallowed my sarcasm and said, "I can't believe you would treat a Brother that way."

"I am sincerely sorry about that Brother Chris. I will make it up to you. Heck, all that those people had was salads anyway."

"That may be true, but when I buy you lunch, I am buying lunch for a family of four, including the dog and the cat. Last month it was like I was buying for the neighbors too."

"But I take you to a higher class and more expensive places. Don't you remember Brother?"

"Oh really, is that so? If that is true can you explain how Sonic Drive-in fit into that definition?"

"OK, you got me on that one. I guess I need to buy lunch a few times in a row to make us even again."

"Sounds good to me. Then I love you again, My Brother. So, where are you planning on taking me today?"

"My niece told me about a place that she goes to all the time. It's all you can eat Mexican food place."

"Uh Oh, it's not Pancho's, is it?"

"Yup. How did you know? I hear it is awful good. My mouth was just watering listening to her talk about all the great food they have."

"Well, it's not my favorite Mexican food place. But I hear that you can eat until you fall out of your chair. Seems like you will fit in perfectly." Honestly, as long as he was buying, I wasn't going to worry about it.

We walked in the door of Pancho's and were greeted with enthusiastic smiles. These workers had no idea what was coming. It didn't take long before they escorted us to the serving line. John grabbed two trays and proceeded to order two of everything. There was every type of enchilada, chalupa, and taco available in both beef or chicken. I think I even counted four or five different cheeses, John's favorite. Another section of the buffet had pinto and borracho beans, Spanish rice, and all the freshly made corn and flour tortillas you could want. We found a variety of bright-colored salsas, hot sauce, pico de gallo, and fresh jalapenos at the guacamole bar. There was also a variety of tamales, sizzling beef and chicken fajitas, and fresh hot sopapillas and honey for dessert.

They all kept smiling as John filled up his trays with two mountains of food. They even helped him carry them to our table. I followed along with my plate and a half of enchiladas. We had to sit at a table for four just to house all the food. Sure enough, we had, as always, quite a few diners checking us out as they walked by our table. Immediately John noticed the flag on the table and realized that you could raise it or lower it. He looked over at me with a questioning look, but before I could explain it to him, Janie, our server approached our table. She explained to John that if he wanted any more food, all he had to do is raise the flag, and she would bring it to him. John's eyes got as big as a kid coming down to a room full of presents on Christmas morning.

I told her that I doubted that we would be raising the flag considering how much he already had in front of him, and she nodded in agreement. Oh, how wrong I can sometimes be. He went into deep silence, and as I ate, I could only marvel at how fast that man could eat. He wasn't messy or sloppy. He was just efficient, with no wasted motion and no talking. Taking advantage of his silence, I talked about Lodge and some proposals that were going to be voted on at Grand Lodge this year. He just nodded and grunted every once in a while. I don't know if he really heard me or not.

John leaned over the table to raise the flag. Janie appeared within what seemed like seconds. She must have been close by waiting for John to give her the signal.

"Hi, Darlin' I'd like some more of them delicious enchiladas and hot and fresh tortillas. Just go ahead and surprise me, I already know that I like all them types of enchiladas ya'll make here."

She seemed a little surprised as she glanced at all the empty plates. She was probably thinking how could this man could possibly want anything else to eat. (I know, because that is exactly what I was thinking). She asked if she could take some dishes away from the table as she pulled the flag down. She grabbed the empty plates, handed them to the busboy, and hurried off to get the food. By the time she got back, John had the flag up again. This time he asked for some more fajitas and pico de gallo. Janie's expression had changed from amusement to puzzled as she delivered John his order and pulled the flag down again.

After she walked away, I saw her out of the corner of my eye talking to the manager, who shook his head in disbelief. I could hear him laughing as Janie told him what John had eaten so far. She glanced back at our table and realized that John had raised the flag again! The entire walk back to the table, she just shook her head. John didn't notice because he was busy eating his second helping of enchiladas. She wasn't smiling this time as John asked for a couple more enchiladas.

As she left, John commented that she seemed to be a little tense. I told him that he was working her to death, having her walk back and forth and back and forth. She came back and set the plate down in front of him, but when she left, she took the flag with her! He just sat there with a lost look on his face.

I knew what he was thinking. He was worried that he wouldn't be able to order anything else, and that scared the bejeezus out of him. He was still eating, and it didn't look like he was gonna get finished any time soon. On the other hand, I had finished my sensible meal, and rather than just sit there and watch him eat, I decided to resume the conversation.

"I have a couple of things to tell you about, OK?" He nodded slightly, so I continued. "My nephew is going to get his third degree in a couple of weeks. His Lodge has agreed to allow me to be the one who raises him to the Sublime Degree of a Master Mason. It is really a great feeling to be a part of the beginning of his Masonic journey."

John looked up from his plate and raised his eyebrows. "Beginning?"

"Yes, my Brother, I do mean the beginning. Do you remember the night you were raised? Was it not the beginning of the rest of your life? Was it not a turning point in your life? Looking back, was it not the night that the world as you knew it changed?" In between bites, John nodded.

"Mine too, Brother John. I know I changed. Not drastically right at first, but it started out slowly like a snowball rolling down a hill, getting bigger and bigger the faster it goes. I know that I am a very different person now than I was before that night. The same on the outside, a little older looking, but very different on the inside. The change was so gradual that my wife didn't even see it at first. I just remember that one day she realized it. She's the one that pointed it out. After that discussion, I began to think about the observations she made, rolling them over in my mind for a couple of days. I also realized how different I was on the inside. Absorbing the principles and lessons of our Craft over the years had made me a much better man than I was before. I could feel it. I always thought I was a good man, but my thinking had changed. The way I looked at other people and other things had changed. Heck, me and the big guy have become pretty close over the years. I don't mean the Grand Master, although he's a great man. I mean the Supreme Architect of the Universe. The most significant big guy. We talk all the time, especially going to and from work and on the road. I don't even have time for the radio. Between our conversations and going over the esoteric work while driving, I don't have time to listen anymore. My Grandfather once told my mother that if she ever saw a man driving down the road and talking to himself, he was either crazy or a Mason. I now know what he meant by that. Masonry has brought out things in me that I never knew existed. Things I never knew I could do, things I would never have attempted ...... what about you, John?"

John nodded in agreement. I could tell that he was winding down. The plates in front of him were nearly empty.

"I thought so. I figure it does it to most of us. And you know what? Doing those things makes me very happy. Brother, I am sorry, this is supposed to be your time to talk and me to listen."

Shaking his head, he gave me the rolling sign to go on.

"OK John, thanks. We talked at Lodge last week about how Masonry affects each of us differently. One of the Brothers spoke about a trip he took a few years ago with his wife and kids to Washington and New York. Their car had broken down, and they had to use all the rest of the money they had for the trip to get the car fixed. They had no credit cards and had no way to get any money. They were in a desperate situation. He called a Masonic Lodge in the Virginia town they were in for help. A Brother he had never met came and met him, and after establishing that he was a Brother Mason, he asked him what he needed. He said he only needed 50 or 60 dollars to get enough gas to get back home and to get some bread and bologna to eat on the way. The Brother gave him $200.00 and told him to send it back to him when he could afford it. He told me that it was one of the most moving moments of his life. That day he was humbled by a fellow Brothers' generosity, and he gained a life-long friend.

Another Brother stated that when he gets home from work, he is so tired he doesn't want to do anything. That includes coming to Lodge on meeting nights. But as soon as he walks through the door of the Lodge, all of the exhaustion just goes away. These are things that all of us as Masons can relate to because this is how it is.

On the negative side, as a Mason, I see some things going on in our country or in the world, and I am dumbfounded. We have people who are supposed to be Godly and spiritual who are leaders and members of different religious organizations who cannot even tolerate one another. They can't even mind their own house. Instead, they have to attack others as if that makes them superior to who they are attacking. One group accuses another of being a cult, and another says that no one except those that believe as they do will meet God in Heaven. Others are calling for the death and destruction of all those who believe differently than they do, all in the name of God. What the hell are they thinking Brother John? All of them thinking that only *they* are right, and are totally convinced of their moral and spiritual superiority. (a sad look on his face shaking his head slightly)

Are they so blinded by their attempts at exclusivity that they can't see their ignorance? Heck they even attack us because we don't take sides. And yet we Masons meet in Lodge and in public, all different ages, races, backgrounds, interests, and spiritual beliefs and not one antagonistic word, not one sarcastic remark, not one harsh or hurtful thought or deed is exchanged between Brothers about anyone's religious beliefs because no one cares what you believe. We only care that you DO believe. This is the specialness of Masonry. Ever since the very moment when man has known right from wrong there have been men who stand up for honor and integrity and who stand up for what is right no matter what. As long as there has been evil in the world there have been good men who fight for what is right, for man's freedom to choose, to worship, to express himself. They have been known by many different names throughout the centuries but their actions and deeds have all been consistently the same. At this particular period in history they are called Masons. This is why I love this Fraternity and what it stands for."

I paused to take a much-needed breath and he was grinning from ear to ear. I looked around and realized that several people were watching us. "John, why didn't you tell me I was too loud?" I asked as I lowered my voice to almost a whisper.

"Heck Brother Chris," John said as he reached over to the empty table next to us and grabbed the flag and hoisted it on our table. "You were so wound up I don't think I could have slowed you down. Besides I had my mouth full and I couldn't talk."

"I appreciate you not trying to Brother John. Anyway, I started out telling you about being a part of my nephew's Masters Degree and I got kinda carried away but I am sure excited to go up there and do it. Every time I get to work in a new Brothers Degrees it's like living mine all over again. I am sorry I went on so long, I'm pretty much talked out except to say how happy I am for my nephew for getting right to his work and getting it, all done. It's an extra measure of good feeling when it's a family member who is beginning his travels. I am looking forward to a lot of years of

Masonic communication between us and I sure am proud to call him my Brother."

Before John could say anything, Janie appeared and apologized to John for taking his flag and asked him what she could get him.

"I just wanted to tell you what a great job you did and to thank you." Her expression went from mildly irritated to puzzled to a big smile. While she was enjoying his praise, John got a sad puppy dog look on his face. "Could I have a couple more of those enchiladas? I really like them."

She laughed out loud and slapped him playfully on the arm and headed towards the kitchen. When she got back she had a plate with at least six enchiladas on it. She set it in front of him and gave him a little hug. "Now honey, you just raise that flag if you need anything else."

I was shaking my head in disbelief as John sat there chewing on his enchiladas with a self-absorbed contented smile on his face. "I will never understand how you can make someone mad at you and then manage to get in their good graces once again so easily. It blows my mind."

"It's my charisma, don't be jealous. Green isn't a good color on you Brother." John said with a grin between bites of enchilada.

I just shook my head and raised the flag. I've known John long enough not to argue with him.

"Aha, you talked so much you got hungry again, right?"

Janie saw the flag again and came over expecting to talk to John. Still eating, John pointed at me. I asked her what kinds of desserts they had and she told me they had sopapillas, Mexican custard, cheesecake, and Mexican sweetbreads.

"OK, give me three orders of Sopapillas and plenty of honey to go with them, four slices of sheesecake, a couple of cups of the Mexican sustard, and about a half dozen of the sweetbreads. Oh, and all of it to go except one slice of sheesecake."

I heard John choking and sputtering. Before he could say anything, I wrote the word **PAYBACK** on my napkin and slid it across the table in front of him and fixed him with a stern stare. When John looked up from the napkin, "You're buying dessert for the guys at the shop because you are such a charismatic guy and they really appreciate it."

Well John threw back his head and laughed out loud. "That's what I like about you Brother Chris," John said as he paid our bill. "The payback is almost as much fun as the prank itself."

We walked out together with Janie beside us. She thanked John with a big smile. Apparently, he made up for being a pain in the rear with some rather larger than normal tip. And that's the way it ended. Janie was happy with her tip. The guys at the shop were happy with their dessert. I was happy because I didn't have to pay for any of it. And of course, John was happy because his belly was full. Ain't it great when a plan comes together? Happy Thanksgiving to all.

ARE YOU AFRAID TO SHOW YOUR MASONIC PRIDE?

You know, it's a wonder my wife hasn't just changed the locks on the house one night while I was gone to some Masonic function. I will tell you that I have driven up to my house halfway more than once, expecting to see all my clothes sitting in the middle of the driveway in a big pile. A couple of times when the garage door wouldn't open when I pressed my car remote, I had a moment of uneasiness thinking that I had been to one meeting too many. I tell you this after trying to explain to Pam why I needed to give up a Saturday to help my Brother John Deacon do a Master Mason Degree. Heck, a Masters Degree only takes a couple of hours, so what's the big deal. Well.... I had to drive four hours just to get there and, of course, four hours back when we were done. If you think I could get away from John without having a meal with him, this has to be the first time you have read a John Deacon story.

Soooooo, after getting that one-eyed raised eyebrow look as I headed out the door, I was a little nervous about trying to get back in the house late that night. Naaaaaaah, I thought as I drove down the road, *she wouldn't do that.... would she? Oh crap, I need to stop thinking about it. I don't want to mess around and attract it into reality.* Maybe I was overreacting a little bit, but I sometimes feel bad about spending so much time working in Masonry. I guess it's really all in my mind because Pam has never actually gotten angry about the amount of time I spend with my Masonic commitments. I wonder if I am part of the majority in this situation or in the minority. I suspect it's the former, but I'm not totally sure.

I pulled up in front of the Lodge and immediately I was impressed with what I saw. The building was a very old one-story rock masonry structure that at one time had been two stories. It was not very big, but it had a lot of *character* if you know what I mean. When I walked in the front door, several Brothers were sitting at the tables drinking coffee. Back in the corner, scarfing down a taco, was Big John Deacon. Having a mouthful of tortilla and eggs, John waved me over to a chair opposite him. I shook hands with all the Brothers as I made my way to him.

I slid into an empty chair, "So, why did I have to drive 200 miles to help you do a degree?"

"For several reasons, Brother Chris," he replied between bites. "First, we needed help because we didn't have enough people. Secondly, it's been a long time since I have conferred a Masters Degree, so you are going to do it."

"Wait a darn minute, I have to confer this thing? You might have told me so I could go over it a couple of times. You couldn't find a Brother within 200 miles that knows how to confer a Masters Degree?"

John snapped back, "Calm down for a second; the other reason I needed you to come up here is that I am not going to be able to come down your way this month, and I had some things I wanted to talk to you about. But we've got to do this degree first." John got up and led everyone into the Lodge.

As it turned out, they didn't need me as bad as John anticipated. These guys were excellent, and the Brother who was raised got an outstanding degree. The Grand Chaplain was in attendance and gave the most beautiful Bible presentation I have ever heard. When he finished, there was not a dry eye in the room. Just before the Lodge was closed, every Brother was given an opportunity to stand up and address the new Brother. I had seen this done at another Lodge, and I really liked it. Some Brothers simply congratulated the newly raised Brother while others stood and implored him to be a student of the Craft. Others gave him serious advice or delivered words of encouragement. It was good to hear the Brothers one by one welcoming this new Brother to the Fraternity. Predictably, after the Lodge was closed, we all retired to a local eatery called Big Dawg Build Your Own Burger.

Now that name could give you the impression of some greasy dive, but it was really an amazing-looking place. Their main claim to fame was their huge burgers, and because there is no commercial bun made to fit the large patties. They bake their own buns. After you decide how big a burger you want, you go down the line and add all the extras like cheese and any and all the veggies you want. I have never seen so much stuff you could put on a burger. This was going to be interesting for sure.

There were eight of us in all, and John was, not surprisingly, at the front of the line. On the menu was (more for novelty than anything else) a two-and-a-half-pound hamburger. I'll never forget the amusement on the counter girl's face when John ordered it. That amusement slowly turned to shock as she moved down the line adding all the extras to those huge buns, the burger's buns, not John's. When they got to the end where his humongous beef patty was waiting to be added, she shook her head in disbelief. That thing had to weigh at least four or five pounds. Heck, it stood almost 6 inches tall altogether.

I could see three different kinds of cheese, lettuce, tomatoes, bell peppers, pickles, jalapenos, cucumbers, purple onions, and avocado from where I was about fourth in line. I don't know how John got them to do it, but there were slices of baked potato on top of his burger too. I just about laughed out loud when I saw the wad of crinkle-cut fries they piled up around that monster of a burger. John talked the drink girl out of a big cup and a whole pitcher of iced tea. John looked anxious with anticipation as he set out to find us all a table. I lost track of John for a few minutes while I ordered my burger, which looked pretty puny compared to Johns. I grabbed my drink and set out to find him.

All I had to do is follow the gaze of all the shocked diners looking at John's hamburger. He motioned for me to sit down across from him as he looked around self-consciously at all the people staring at him. "Heck, you'd think these people had never seen a man eat a burger before," John said in a low voice.

"Oh, they've seen plenty of men eating burgers before, but they have never seen a man eat a whole side of beef in one sitting before." John scowled at me but couldn't say anything because he was already into his third bite.

The rest of the Brothers, including the new Master Mason, finally got to the table and sat down. They all commented concerning John's burger, which was disappearing at a steady rate, as were the fries. We all made small talk as we ate. The other diner's rubber necked John to see if he would eat all of his meal. I could have saved them the trouble and really shocked them by telling them that not only was he going to finish the burger and the fries, but he was probably going to have dessert afterward. Finally, John took the last bite, and as he did, spontaneous applause broke out around the room. I remember thinking, *don't these people have a life?*

At that moment, John made the quote of the day as far as I was concerned. He leaned back in his chair and fixated on the new Master Mason with a steady stare. With a slight smile and the tone of a proud parent getting ready to share a profound experience with his child, "You are so lucky. You have sooo much really neat stuff to learn."

It was such a simple a statement but so true that every Brother at the table smiled and nodded in agreement. It was a nice moment for everyone, and the new Master Mason grinned and assured John that he was ready to learn. With that, the Brothers said their goodbyes and headed for their cars one by one. Not John, of course. Oh no. He got the attention of the waitress and asked for a big bowl of Banana Pudding. At first she thought he was kidding and then realizing he wasn't. She hurried off to the kitchen to get his dessert.

"So, what was so important that I needed to drive all this way to hear?"

"Brother Chris, you know how I am always thinking about how non-Masons perceive our Fraternity and why their perceptions are what they are. I honestly don't know why they are so hostile towards us, but I have done some research. It seems to boil down to two main groups. The first are those who repeat things they have read or heard from someone else but have not taken the time to learn the truth for themselves. In this group is a high percentage of radical religious fundamentalists and some mainstream religions who consider Masons and Masonry as being contrary to their beliefs due to one of our basic principles of accepting good men who believe in God regardless of their particular faith. They fill their followers' heads with false information as well as outright lies concerning our Fraternity. The other group are those former Brothers who are disgruntled at something or someone in the Fraternity. They have dropped out and sought to make money by making the Fraternity out to be secretive or subversive. They claim to *reveal* these so-called subversive activities and secrets even though they know them not to be true.

Not surprisingly, there are not very many of these disgruntled former Brothers. Heck, Brother Chris, I have read many Anti-Masonic books and papers and have yet to find a speck of truth in any of their accusations or claims. Of course, you, I, and every other Mason knows that they are not true, and if any of those who make these ridiculous claims ever became Masons, they would know how silly they had been. I say all of this because I think that sometimes we actually help these people in their desire to hurt us and discredit us by the way we act around them."

John shook his head, "Brother Chris, I am sorry that I got off on such a rant because what I really wanted to tell you was something that happened to me last week. I was in a store, and I noticed the man in line behind me was wearing a Masonic Ring. I caught his eye and asked, 'So, you're a Mason, right?'

Brother Chris, you should have seen the shocked look appear on his face, and then I saw out of the corner of my eye he slid his hand in his pocket so I couldn't see his ring. The first thing I thought was that he was not a Mason and was wrongly wearing the ring. So I asked him what the name of his Lodge was. He just looked at me warily, so I told him that I was a Mason and my Lodge's name. He let out a big breath, told me his Lodge's name, and showed me his dues card. By that time, it was my turn to check out, but I waited for him outside. I was really puzzled and wanted to ask him why he was ashamed to admit that he was a Brother. Darned if he didn't look like he was offended, and he said, 'I am not ashamed to admit that I am a Mason.'

Well, I gave him a long steady look and asked him why he tried to hide his ring when I asked him if he was a Mason. He had no answer to provide me with. He looked down at the ground for a few seconds before finally admitting that he was worried that someone might say something bad about Masons. He just didn't want to get into an argument with anyone about it and said that he remembered something that he heard that we weren't supposed to argue with anyone about the Fraternity anyway.

I told him, 'That's a cop-out, and you know it. Did you ever think that when you act like you're hiding something, that's what makes people suspicious of us?' Before he could answer, I asked him, 'This being Texas, are you a Cowboys fan?'

'Heck yes!'

'Well, if you worked for the Cowboys organization, you'd be so proud that you would be telling everyone you see, wouldn't you? You would want everyone to know.'

'Oh yeah, I sure would.'

I looked at him sideways and said to him, 'I can tell you, my Brother, that if you were as unenthusiastic about being a part of the Cowboys as you seem to be of being a Mason, I don't think they would keep you around very long.'

He blurted out,' But I am proud to be a Mason. I like everything about it. I like being part of what Masonry stands for and what it does.'

I just looked at him and shook my head. 'My Brother, you are talking the talk, but you just ain't walking the walk. You can't have one without the other. It just don't work that way. Masonry is either your life or it's not.'

He said something under his breath that I made him repeat because I wanted to make sure what he said. He wrongly noted that Masons were not supposed to talk about Masonry to non-Masons anyway.

Hellfire Brother Chris, I just about blew a cork, but I kept my cool. In the calmest voice I could muster, I told him to 'step right over to my trusty stead Ol' Blackie and let me haul out my Law Book. That way you can show me where it says that Masons aren't supposed to talk to non-Masons about Masonry. I just happen to believe that if it doesn't say in this book that I can't do it, then it's authorized.'

Brother Chris, he went to stuttering and stammering. I had him dead to rights, and he knew it. I wasn't about to let him go. He was so confused he didn't know what to say, but that's part of the problem, isn't it? Confusion reigns, and no one knows what to say or how to say it. It's no wonder people think all kinds of weird things about us. What are they to think when we can't explain who and what we are. Heck, we are not like some club that just does charity. We are a system of teaching, a pathway to moral and spiritual knowledge, and people just don't get that. Hell, most of us don't even get it. We have a very small percentage of Masons who are students, real students of the craft. Then we have a larger percentage who are students in training reading, learning, and gaining important knowledge. But the sad part is that we have an overwhelming percentage of Brothers who bask in the exclusivity and mystery of our Fraternity, with no real clue what they are really a part of. They have taken from it, and all they care to give is the barest minimum which may be enough fulfillment for them but doesn't, in the long run, benefit them or Masonry to the extent that it could and should."

John was talking faster, and of course, the quicker he spoke, the louder he got. I needed to reign him in if I could, so just as he stopped to take a breath, I put out both hands, "Whoaaaaaa up there, Brother John."

He sputtered a couple of times, "Whaaaaaaat?"

"I hear you. I agree with you, but what happened with the Brother in the store?"

John gave me a blank look for a couple of seconds and finally said, "Oh yeah, sorry, got sidetracked. Well, I just told him that if he was proud to be a Mason like he said, he would be calm and comfortable and happy to talk with anyone about Masonry, no matter who it was. But more importantly, no matter what the other person may say in response. I told him that he ought to stick out his chest with pride and tell anyone who will listen about this great organization we belong to. I don't mean that he should get in people's faces and force them to listen. Still, when asked, he should be able and *happy* to respond to any questions about Masonry and correct misleading statements about us with positive information instead of defensive excuses. It's all about showing your pride in being a Mason. How will anyone want to emulate you if you don't show pride in what you are doing? I knew I was making him feel bad, but he needed to hear this. You know me, Brother Chris, I gotta say what I gotta say."

There was no way to get a word in, so I just nodded. I didn't want to even try to interrupt him when he was delivering one of his passionate speeches.

"Then the Brother said something about it being so confusing. Well, duhhhhh, of course, it's confusing. How could you ever believe that such a beautiful system of moral and spiritual teachings designed to purify your mind and soul would be easy? First of all, if moral and spiritual growth were easy, we surely would not have near the corruption and evil and social unrest we have in the world. Do you not think that Masonry is needed in this world? Do you know men who SHOULD be Masons? Then why on earth wouldn't you find a way to talk to them? You need to consider that it is for their good as much as for the good of Masonry. Don't be afraid to talk about it. (finally, he paused to take a breath)

Shoot, Brother Chris, when I got done talking he said he was wore out. But he also said that he understood and was not going to be afraid to talk about Masonry anymore."

"I know what he means John, I'm worn out too."

Then John realized that his pudding had been sitting in front of him for several minutes and was getting warm, so he totally ignored me and dug into his dessert. I just sat there and watched him devour his pudding thinking about his passion for Masonry and that it was well worth the trip up here to listen to him. The bill came; John picked it up and looked at me. I looked back at him, and John stared, and I stared back until finally he smiled and shrugged. John handed a confused waitress his card.

As we walked to our trucks, I told John I thought he was right in all he said and that we needed more Brothers with his passion and love for Masonry. He assured me there were plenty more out there but agreed that we needed more. He thanked me for coming and informed me that he would withhold any more newsletter material until I started paying for lunch again. I said I would think about it and shook his hand. As I walked away, I remember thinking about how comforting that familiar grip was. One small token between two Brothers says so much.

Then my mind shifted back to driving up to my house and seeing my clothes sitting in the yard. I have to stop thinking about it, I know, but if I didn't feel a little guilty, then it wouldn't be popping back in my mind, right? You know, sometimes it's Masonry that keeps me sane during this insane time we are living in. It sure helps me see that I am on the side of the good guys. Guys who think the way I do, have the same love of family, country, and a sense of what is right and wrong. I know that this Gentle Fraternity, its teachings, and lessons have made me a better man and continue to do so. Maybe Pam sees that, and perhaps that's why she gives me the *one-eyed raised eyebrow* look but leaves my clothes in the closet. I'll need to thank her for that. I surely couldn't do any of this without her.

Until next time be thankful for what you have and fight for what is good and what is right. And Brothers, don't forget to thank the special person in your life for being supportive.

The Generation Gap, What a Bunch of "B.S."

It was going to be a good night, hopefully. For a year, I tried to talk to my Brother John into coming into town and attend a meeting at my Lodge. Well, he had finally agreed and was supposed to show up tonight. I checked the bank account to make sure we could buy enough to feed him and put the Stewards on high alert. After I told Doug and Tim who was coming to dinner, they started stressing out, worrying about what to serve and how much food to make. Once the shock had worn off a bit, I heard them grumbling about hazardous duty pay. Heck, they don't get paid now, but I understood their worry.

John came by the shop to ride with me to the meeting. We made small talk on the way, mostly about what happened at the Grand Lodge earlier in the month. John was in a pretty good mood. He kept asking me what was on the menu for dinner. I told him I didn't know, but our Stewards were the best. I was sure he would have trouble keeping his eyes open during the meeting after filling his belly. I don't know how they did it, but Doug and Tim had come up with the perfect dinner for John. They must have been reading John's column and knew what to fix. When we crossed the Lodge threshold, the distinct smell of fried chicken was the first thing that met us. I thought I saw John's eyes roll back in his head.

I introduced John all around, but it was clear that our Stewards were at the top of his buddy list. The food was ready soon, and the Worshipful Master asked Bro Vic, our Chaplain, for a prayer. The WM announced that our visitor would be first in line, which was unnecessary because John was already grabbing a plate, no, two plates. He had no trouble filling both. The guys had done well. There was a massive mound of fresh fried chicken, and next to that was a big bowl of mashed potatoes and gravy. One of Toni and Olaf's fantastic salads was next, followed by some mouth-watering dinner rolls. John ended up with so much food on the plates that he had to come back to get his drink and eating utensils. John sat down, and his table filled up quickly with curious guys. Some of them attempted to strike up a conversation with John, which was doomed to failure. The most they got out of him was a nod and a grunt from time to time. It didn't take John long to finish off the first two plates and head back for more. I have to say it was pretty darn good, and I was starting to worry that I wouldn't be able to stay awake in the meeting. Not surprisingly, he went back for the third time, and I think it was the first time that there was not a speck of food of any kind left at a stated meeting. I saw several of the Brothers shaking their heads in disbelief as we all wandered into the Lodge Room for the meeting.

Patrick assumed the East and opened the Lodge. Everyone was introduced, including his roundness. John was thanked for making the Stewards look good. John, carrying at least thirty pounds extra with considerable effort, hauled himself to his feet. After being recognized, "Worshipful Master, these fellers don't need me to make them look good. Heck, that was probably the best meal I have ever had in a Lodge and one of the best anywhere. I make a motion that they are given the title of Stewards for Life."

Immediately Doug and Tim started waving their hands and shaking their heads, and I thought I heard a second from someone. Luckily the WM headed the motion off at the pass and thanked Brother John again. After the pledges to the United States Flag and Texas's State Flag, the meeting settled down into a normal pace. Most of the regular business was handled, and we came to the part of the meeting where we always have a Masonic education program presented by our *Light Brigade Committee*. Brother Brad had the program for this meeting. He prepared a different and unique program titled *The Generation Gap. What a Bunch of B.S.* None of us really knew what he was channeling until he set up a CD player for music.

Brad then asked the Worshipful Master if he could rearrange where some of the Brethren were seated in the Lodge. After getting permission, he moved the youngest Brothers and sat next to the oldest Brothers. He explained that the generation gap was created by advertisers who created the message that what was ok for a previous generation was not good for the next because it was old and the new generation needed its own identity. Brad wanted to prove his point by using music. He prepared two songs from each of the past seven decades. He then read some of the lyrics from the two songs from the 1940s and then played the songs so we could hear the lyrics in the songs. He did the same thing for every decade to the present. His contention, which was evident early on, was that the words to songs have remained pretty much the same in seventy years, only the packaging had changed. It was an excellent program, and as the music was played in each decade, I looked at the Brothers who were in their teens and early twenties during that decade. There was pure nostalgia on their faces. I was lost in memories of several of the decades. From the looks of many of the other Brothers, I was not the only one. I thought it was fantastic, but I had no idea of the surprise Brad had for us.

Brad reiterated that the generation gap was mainly made up. Then he asked the Worshipful Master to raise the Lodge, "If you want to know the power that music has to unite us ...." he pressed the play button, and immediately all the Brethren turned, placed their hands on their hearts, and faced the flag as the *Star-Spangled Banner* played. It was very moving, and then to accommodate our two British Brethren, he played while singing, *God Save the Queen.*

I will tell you that many Brothers wiped their eyes as they applauded the program. Brother Brad wasn't through, "I want each and every one of you to grasp the hand of the person sitting next to you with the strong grip of the Lion of the tribe of Judah, and I don't care if they have long hair, short hair, gray hair, or no hair, look them in the eye and know, *this is my Brother.* After all, in the life of an immortal soul, what difference does a few decades make?"

Wow! What an ending. It didn't take long to cover the remaining business and tell a couple of funny stories to send each Brother home smiling before closing the Lodge. I knew there was dessert to have before we left. I hoped John was not starving (wishful thinking) and we could get on home. No such luck, as he made a hard-right turn coming out the Lodge Room door as if he was being pulled by some unseen force towards that big chocolate cake on the counter. All I could do is relax and enjoy it because he wasn't leaving until he had a lot of that cake. It was a darn good cake.

By the time John had finished with his socializing and eating, it was getting pretty late. The only consolation is that I had time to finish transcribing all my minutes which put me ahead of the game for the week. We said goodbye to everyone and started heading back to John's truck. The cake had me all pumped up, but he was strangely quiet. When I asked him what the problem was, he got real serious sounding, "Brother Chris, I cannot tell you how happy I am that I came to visit your Lodge on this particular night."

"Why is that, John."

There were a few seconds of silence before he spoke, and when he did, it was in that slow and deliberate way he talks when something has seriously affected him. "That program that Brother Brad gave tonight was one of the most profound lectures I have ever heard. It was completely non-Masonic in content but at the same time completely Masonic in meaning. It was dripping with the kind of symbolism and lessons that defines Masons and Masonry."

Well, I was a little confused, but I let him talk. (like I had much of a choice).

"The allusions to Brothers being *on the Square* with each other no matter what our packaging, old or young, rich or poor, strong or weak, was readily obvious. I saw that most of the Brothers in the Lodge could see that right off the bat. But to the Brother whose mind was prepared to receive them, there were some not so obvious messages and lessons. There was a warning about making sure to always look past the obvious (the internal, not the external) in dealing with people and situations in life, to not judge a book by its cover. The lyrics of one song, 'call on me Brother, if you need a hand… we all need somebody to lean on.' Not about Masons and Masonry at all…. yet it totally describes Masons and Masonry; precisely what we are and who we are.

I saw the Brothers being transported back in time. I saw them smiling at the music, and I saw them mouthing the words. I saw their foot tapping to the beat, and I saw the tears of fond memories forming at the corners of their eyes. Oh yes, the Brothers listened, and the Brothers understood. Some of them more than others, but all in their own way. And it affected me in a big way. It took me back to times and places from long ago; good times and bad times both. I realized that today, all these people, including myself, are pretty darn near the same as 50, 60, and 70 years ago. We all have the same basic thoughts, dreams, and needs as we did back then. Even our kids have the same concerns as we did. It was great in so many ways, and I won't forget this night. Heck, I didn't want it to stop. Then Brother Brad played the National Anthem, and I lost it. I haven't cried in a while, Brother, but I did then, and I wasn't the only one. Then to top it all off, he asked every Brother to shake the hand of the Brother next to him with the strong grip of a Master Mason. It was a fitting way to end a fantastic program."

Dear Readers,

I just sat there in awe. I have to confess that I was humbled and

ashamed that I had not seen all John had seen. It had affected me also but not to the extent that it impacted John. The truth be known, I was a little angry at myself for not seeing what he saw. I guess I was just a little jealous of his level of understanding.

John must have sensed my disappointment in my silence, "You know, Brother Chris, everyone sees things just a little different than anyone else. The things I see tonight I might not see another time where you might. This really is the beauty of our system of freethinking. Masonry doesn't tell people what to think or; it to think; it instead gives them the tools to think, reason, create, and discover on their own."

I smiled, "Thanks for trying to make me feel better. But I still wish I had seen the things you did. But now that you have said them, I can see them now."

"Brother Chris, you guys should do that program for a family night or somewhere where everyone can see it. It is something everyone should see."

John thanked me once again for inviting him as we shared the grip of a Master Mason. I told him he needed to come back after we replenished the kitchen and the treasury. John just smiled knowingly.

Y'all have a great month, and keep living your Masonry.

At the Flagstop and All Good Men Deserve a Chance

The phone had been ringing off the wall all morning long. I couldn't remember a day that had been this busy. We even had the boss up front helping us. Roger called out that the call on hold was for me. As I reached for it, Roger said, "I think it's your friend John Deacon." I shook my head as I picked it up. John called earlier to tell me that he was coming by and wanted to have lunch. I told him I was too busy to have lunch. I really hated to miss it because I hadn't written my article yet. I figured John must have broken down someplace, it was going to be a long afternoon.

"Hello John, what's up?"

"Lunch is what's up!" John growled. It sounded like his mouth was full of something. "I'm sitting here eating by myself, and it ain't near as much fun as arguing with you."

Cautiously I replied, "I would like to take that as a compliment, but I told you I couldn't get away."

In a whiny voice, John objected. "But I hate to eat alone, and people are staring at me."

I felt a tap on my shoulder, I turned, and Leonard said, "Go eat with him real quick. He's liable to get into trouble if you don't show up."

It had slowed a bit, so I nodded and asked John where he was. He let out a big whoop that hurt my ear. I am sure it got him some nasty looks from anyone close to him.

"I am right here at that place you are always bragging about, the Flagstop Cafe."

"That sounds great, John. I'll be right there. Don't eat all the food before I get there."

Dear Readers,

The Flagstop Cafe is a tiny country café that has been added on to a convenience store and gas station right on the side of Interstate Highway - 10 outside San Antonio. I brag about it because they have the best home-cooked meals, like fried Chicken, chicken fried steak, meatloaf, pot roast, fried fish, all kinds of hamburgers, and yes, enchiladas. Diners can choose side dishes like mashed potatoes, okra, and macaroni and cheese. The thing I love the most is their philly cheesesteak sandwich. It is one of the best cheesesteak sandwiches I have ever had. The meat has a wonderful flavor. They lay about six slices of that monterey jack cheese, a bunch of grilled bell peppers and onions on it, and slip the whole thing onto a hoagie roll. I guarantee that it is truly addictive.

Walking into the door, I was stressing a little because this was way too close to the shop. More than likely, I was going to see one of our customers. I sure hoped John was in a calm mood. The first thing I encountered was two cowboys looking across the dining room in John's direction and mumbling in low tones to each other. As I passed them, I heard one say to the other, "Emmitt, I've got ten dollars that says he can't eat all that food in front of him." I glanced back and saw Emmitt in deep thought. For a moment, I thought about going back and taking that bet. But my Masonic values wouldn't let me take advantage of him. Instead, I called out, *"Take the bet!"* I don't know if he did, but I was sure that no matter what was in front of John, he would eat it all.

When I got back to where John was, I couldn't believe my eyes. I almost went back to tell Emmitt to get his money back. There was food everywhere on the table, and he had already consumed about half of it. John had a big plate of fried chicken in front of him, and I don't know what had been on the two empty plates next to that. There were two of the Philly cheesesteaks with French fries sitting there also. I slid into a chair across from him and reached for one of the cheesesteaks, and if I hadn't been as quick as I was, I might have lost part of my hand as John snatched the plate from me.

"My mistake John. I thought you had been a nice Brother and ordered for me. Guess I was wrong."

John snapped, "Not a chance. I didn't know how long you were going to be, so I went ahead and ordered my stuff."

"Oh, I see how it is. Well, just ordering for myself will be the cheapest meal I have ever had with you." John smiled as I headed over to the cashier to order.

The cashier's name was Jessalynn. She and her parents are some of our best customers at the shop. She is a real nice young lady. We like her a lot. She always has something nice to say, until today.

I ordered a cheesesteak for myself and something to drink. Jessalynn started to ring it up. A little red flag went up in my mind; she punched way too many buttons on her machine. Just as I began to say something, Jessalynn said, "That will be $47.23 today." I must have looked like I was going to pass out because she quickly followed with, "Your friend said it was your turn to pay; he is your friend, isn't he?"

I looked over at John as he waved and smiled. I didn't return any pleasantries. I turned back to Jessalynn and paid the ticket muttering something about John being lucky he was my Brother because he was no friend of mine right then. When I sat back down at the table, all John said was, "Well, it is your turn."

"Yeah, right, the problem is that I had to refinance my truck to be able to cover these lunches with you." John seemed to think that was funny for some reason. My cheesesteak showed up, and we ate in silence for a bit. I finished and waited for him to get done. I sure hoped he had something interesting on his mind this month.

I waited while John took a couple of deep breaths and finally, "Brother Chris, we had our official District Deputy Grand Master visit two weeks ago. This year, the Grand Master's message is all about the membership, getting them in, and keeping them once they join. He talked some about not waiting for a man to ask about Masonry but to reach out to a man you know is a good man and tell him why he should be a Mason. I thought a little about what the DDGM said, and you know, it makes sense to do that. Heck, who knows more non-Masons who are good men than we Masons do. We already know who would make good Brothers. I sometimes think that we are convinced that everyone, everywhere, knows who we are. Since some Brothers believe that, we don't say anything to anyone about the Fraternity. They fear that the person might already have a negative opinion. I don't know why we think this, but there's a whole bunch of Brothers that do, who will never approach the good men that they know and tell them about one of the best things that they ever did, being initiated into Masonry.

I did me a little survey over the last two weeks. I have asked so far about fifty men, some I know real well and some I barely know. I asked them what they know about Masonry, and I was shocked that out of fifty guys, barely half knew about the Masons. The other half had no idea who or what Masons are. The half that knew about us, only about half of them knew anything about what we do and who we are. Four of the ones that knew about us had a bad opinion of the Fraternity, and after talking to them for just a couple of minutes, they admitted that they had heard bad things from someone else or had read things about us on social media. None of the men that knew anything about Masonry knew how to become a Mason. Isn't that amazing?"

"Wow, that is amazing, John. That means there are literally thousands and thousands of men out there who might want to be Masons who don't know we exist."

"Right, you are Brother Chris. We need to get out there and talk about the greatest organization in the world. That's what I intend to do from here on out."

"You gotta be careful, John, not to push anyone into filling out a petition. You know it's got to be of their own free will and accord."

John grinned, "Right again, my Brother, but let me give you a hamburger analogy."

"Do you know what analogy means, Brother John?"

John gave me a dirty look and continued, "Like I said, a hamburger analogy. If you went into a restaurant and there was a burger on the menu called the John Deacon Burger but there was no description of it. Nothing was available for you to read about what was in it or on it or what came with it; no information at all. Would you order that burger?"

"Well, if it were called the John Deacon Burger, I already know it would be too dang big to eat in one sitting, or for one person. But not knowing anything about it, I wouldn't buy it because I wouldn't want to waste my money on something I might not like."

John was getting a little louder with excitement, "*Exactly my point, Brother Chris!* The number of men who will be curious enough to ask about Masonry on their own is a heck of a lot less than the ones who might be interested if they were told about Masonry. Especially by a Brother who offers information in conversation with a man he knows is a good candidate for the Fraternity. Do you remember when those movies came out a couple of years ago that had a lot of Masonry in them?"

"Of course, I remember them; who doesn't?"

"Well, the Fraternity got a huge number of men asking about Masonry during that time, and we got a lot of new Brothers out of it. I am saying that telling people about Masonry should be as easy and natural as talking about what you do for a living. In fact, I know a Brother who, when asked what business he is in, responds, 'I am a Mason, but I make my money in the consulting business."

"That's pretty cool, John. It makes perfect sense too. I reckon that maybe I'll start doing that."

"Brother Chris, you might think I am crazy, but I asked a man who I have known for many years this question: 'Have you ever thought about giving some of your time, talents, and wisdom to something that will reward you with happiness, contentment, and much more wisdom?' He looked at me for about 20 seconds, and I could see he was rolling it around in his mind. Then he asked me what I was talking about. When I got through telling him about Masonry, he asked me what he had to do to join. That was pretty cool, and I am looking forward to bringing him to Lodge with me. All I did was share the truth, and he was able to conclude that he wanted to be a part of our great Fraternity."

"That's great, John. I am going to start talking more about the Craft, too, right away. I can't believe I have never thought about it this way before."

"You know, Brother Chris; I think if we just told more good men out there about our great Fraternity, we would have new members all over the place. But if we get them, we have to keep them. That's the other thing I was thinking about. I remembered while I was driving down here today about all the new Entered Apprentices that we have initiated in our Lodge over the past few years and how many never finished their degrees. I know that some were not ready to be Masons and their loss was inevitable, but there were many more who I think we failed. It's also not hard to believe that we may have been unable to live up to what we promised."

I felt my eyebrows raise a bit, "You need to explain that one, John. I am not sure that I fully understand that."

"I can remember a few that we totally ignored after the initiation. Oh heck, we didn't do it on purpose. I remember a couple of Brothers who were not very outgoing, and I suppose now that I think about it a little different than they might have been a little shy or maybe a little self-conscious. I can remember that some of the Brothers thought that they were just anti-social. And you know, we didn't extend the hand of Brotherly love and friendship. Well, they stopped coming, and we never saw them again.

I feel like we failed them, all the Brothers in our lodge didn't do our part to support them. And nope, we didn't follow up either. We just left them alone, and we lost them forever.

There were other Brothers that we failed too. We told them there would be Brothers as ready to give as they would be to receive instruction. They found out that there were very few who would or could provide instruction. We promised them light or Masonic education, and then we gave them instructors who weren't qualified to teach or explain. Again, our fault because we stopped teaching Brothers to be instructors. I wonder just how many would still be or would have continued and finished their work had we done what we promised we would."

John's voice was angry and frustrated and helpless all at the same time. I could see and hear the deep anger coming to the front, and you know when the angry comes, it comes out loud. I glanced around to see if anyone was hearing John. Having been so intently focused on John's words, I hadn't noticed the two cowboys Emmitt and his buddy had sat down at the table next to us. They were looking towards us.

"John, we need to lower the volume a bit cause we are bothering some of the people in here."

Before John could answer, Emmitt said, "You ain't bothering us none." As he said it, Emmitt got up and came over to our table. He sat right down next to John, and his buddy came and sat down next to me. John and I exchanged confused looks as Emmitt said, "You know the big guy here is right. I dang near never came back after I was initiated. If it weren't for a chance meeting with one of my lodge Brothers at a store and him asking me how it was going, I would have never gone back. Heck, they didn't even realize what they did to run me off." Emmitt saw the confusion in our faces.

He held out his hand, "Sorry, my name is Emmitt, and this here is my Lodge Brother Roy." The grip verification was made, and we were instant friends. In fact, I remembered seeing them in a Lodge a couple of times.

Emmitt pulled two ten-dollar bills out of his shirt pocket and said to me, "Thanks for the info. You knew he would eat it all, didn't you?"

"Yup, I sure did," I replied as John looked from Emmitt to me and back, confused.

Roy looked at me and said sarcastically, "Yeah, thanks a lot."

"Sorry, he is a big eater. My advice is to avoid John anywhere close to mealtime. Or at least be able to get your food order in before him. We can never be certain if there will be anything left to order after he does."

John got a little defensive, "Well, there you go again, Brother Chris. Talking bad about me in front of my new friends."

"Just stating the facts, John." Turning to Emmitt, "So you Brothers heard what John was saying?"

"We sure did, and I have myself an opinion on all of that. Some Brothers out there say that we should never say anything about the Fraternity at any time; that's wrong. First of all, there is nothing that says that anywhere. It's all a misinterpretation of the '*of their own free will and accord*' statement. The original intent was not that we shouldn't talk about Masonry, but that's the way it has worked out. We are just not supposed to push anyone into submitting a petition. Once they have all the information, then they need to decide on their own. Back when we had plenty of membership, it didn't really matter, but now it does. We have Lodges about to shut down because they can't pay their bills. And if that ain't bad enough, there's still Lodges out there that are so stubborn and hard-headed that they refuse to raise their dues. Instead, they blame all their troubles on the Grand Lodge. Brothers, if I had my druthers, I would like not to tell anyone about our Fraternity because everyone knew about us and every man wanted to be one of us, but that is just not the case. If we keep going the way we are, we are going to stubborn ourselves out of business. How much worse does it have to be before we pull our heads out and turn this thing around? We don't have to sacrifice anything at all. We have to start talking to good men about this Fraternity we all love. How hard could that be?"

John spoke up, "That was well put, Brother Emmitt; I am glad you said it. How about we all have some dessert and discuss it some more?"

Well, that was my cue to get out of Dodge. I said my goodbyes all around and headed out. As I walked out the door, I looked back to see John waving and…. danged if he hadn't got Emmitt to buy dessert. What a guy.

Remember, all good men deserve the chance to be a Mason. Let's try to make sure that they get that opportunity.

THE BARN DOOR AND GUARDING
THAT WEST GATE

I am a little ashamed to say that I had been so busy that I hadn't even thought about my Brother John Deacon the whole month. But one thing I have found out is that John doesn't let you forget him. I left the shop to go pick up a sandwich for lunch when my cell phone rang. I didn't recognize the number. I still answered it anyway. My mistake, depending on which way you look at it. I heard an animated voice on the other end, "Brother Chris, I just called the shop, and they said you left for lunch. You better not be eating yet cause I'm down here waiting for you to get here."

"Nice of you to let me know beforehand, John," I replied. I started trying to figure out how much money I had in the bank. Having lunch with my rather expensive Brother is considered in my household a significant purchase, especially when I get stuck with the bill.

Realizing that payday was around the corner, I changed course and headed to meet John at a place I hadn't been to in a long time. I wondered how he even found out about the Barn Door. They easily have some of the best steaks I have ever had, and their green garlic salad dressing is fantastic. I got there, and all I had to do is follow the sound of John's booming voice to find his table way back in the corner.

John was confused about the large dispensers of several different kinds of salad dressings on the table. Our server, Shelly, was getting a little exasperated with John and all his questions, "Sir you can use any dressing you wish, as much as you wish, and it doesn't cost any extra."

John smiled and winked, "Oh heck, Darlin, I ain't paying for it anyway. So that don't matter to me. What is your biggest and best steak?"

"Whoa up there, John, maybe we ought to get this '*I ain't paying for this anyway*' thing settled before we start ordering everything on the menu."

"We don't need to be holding up Shelly from doing her work," John said calmly as he motioned to her to keep writing. Shelly complied.

John ordered an appetizer of fried mushrooms, a huge steak, and baked potato with all the fixins. Then just before she turned to get my order, he asked her to bring him a salad for each of the three dressing containers. I just shook my head and asked for the medium sirloin. Instead of a regular baked potato, I told her I wanted one of their specialties called a Tassos potato, a twice-baked potato with jalapenos. It is about the best I have ever had. Right away, John wanted to know about the potato. After receiving a description, he proceeded to order one for himself. Shelly was finally able to turn in our orders, and pretty soon, we were munching on our salads.

John got quiet as he always does when he is concentrating on eating, which for him is truly a spiritual experience. Before he finished all three of his salads, our steaks came. John shifted gears and dug into his plate without missing a beat. Just as he was finishing up, he got a phone call, and it seemed to sadden him.

"Are you OK, Brother John? You look like you just lost your best friend."

"Yup, I have had a bad couple of weeks," he replied sadly, hanging his head in shame. "I just found out that I am on Granddaughter probation."

I was confused already. "What do you mean, Granddaughter probation? I don't understand what that is."

"It's just been a nightmare, Brother Chris. It started a couple of weeks ago when my daughter dropped off my granddaughter so she and I could spend some time together while my wife and daughter went shopping. My granddaughter brought her school books with her to study for a test. Well, she pulled out the study guide with possible questions that might be on the test and asked me if I would help her study. That's when the problems started. She started asking me questions, and I answered as best as I could. After the test, my daughter got a note from the teacher concerning some of my granddaughter's answers. Apparently, I gave her some wrong answers. She got a bad grade, and now I am not allowed to help her with her school work anymore."

"My God, John, how hard were the questions?"

John replied in a whiny voice, "That's the problem, they were really easy, and I don't know what the problem is."

"What kind of questions were they?"

"Well, let's see. One of the questions was, where was the Declaration of Independence signed?"

"That's not hard," I replied.

"I know it's not hard, but the teacher said it was wrong. I don't know what is going on, but everybody knows it was signed at the bottom of the page. What the heck is the matter with you? Why are you looking at me like that?"

I don't know what my expression was but based on John's reaction; I could tell it wasn't normal. I was trying hard not to start laughing. "Uhhhh, John, I think the correct answer is in Philadelphia."

"What do you mean Phila...ohhh (as the realization hit him) they wanted the place. They didn't mean where it was signed on the paper. I understand now. But her question should have been more specific."

I couldn't believe what I was hearing, but I needed to know more.

"What else did your granddaughter miss?"

"Well, there was this question about what is the main reason for divorce, and now that I think about it, maybe marriage was probably not the answer they were looking for, huh?"

"Noooooo, I don't think so," I said, on the verge of losing control because he was still serious. "Any others? I would like to see if I am smarter than a fifth grader." I asked with my voice cracking more out of spite than anything else.... man, this was getting good.

John gave me a serious look, "I don't think the answers they wanted were logical. I remember one test question was 'If you had three apples and four oranges in one hand and four apples and three oranges in another hand, what would you have?' I thought at the time that *very big hands* was a great answer.... heck she even giggled when I said it."

Dear Readers,

I couldn't help it. I started to giggle too, and his face turned red.

John said indignantly, "Well, some of those dad gurn questions were trick questions anyway."

"What do you mean, trick questions?"

"Well, one was 'How do you lift an elephant with one hand?'...... (John leaned in towards me real serious like) Brother Chris I ain't never seen an elephant with one hand."

That's when I lost it. I was laughing so hard that I hurt, and the whole time, John just stared at me like I was crazy. Suddenly, he got a look of terror on his face and said, "Brother Chris, you are not going to put this in your newsletter, are you?"

"Come on, Brother John, this is too good not to share. Don't you agree?"

"Bu..bu..but the Brothers will never take me seriously after this."

"Actually, John, they will probably agree with your answers," I said as I wiped my eyes. "But let's switch gears. Can you give me something I can pass along to the Brothers?"

Well, that did it because he got all serious, "Brother Chris, I have something that is bothering me a whole bunch. I have been needing to talk to you about it. We hear all the time that we should *'Guard Well Our West Gate,'* meaning that we need to make sure that we only allow those who are good men of good character to have the opportunity to become Masons. It is one of the most basic requirements of our Fraternity. Masonry cannot help a man whose heart and mind are not good and true. A man such as that would not have the capacity to absorb or even understand our basic tenets and teachings, much less be able to grow within Masonry's moral structure. But while it is true that all Masons are good men, it is also true that not all Masons can lead."

"What do you mean ...not all Masons can lead?"

"What I am talking about is that while we need to guard the West gate surely, we also need to guard the East as well. Don't look so confused. Let me tell you why. It just so happens that we have at times the wrong Brothers sitting in the East."

"But John, don't you think that every Brother should have an opportunity to be the Master of his Lodge?"

"I sure do, but just because he has the opportunity to seek that position doesn't mean he is qualified to hold that office."

"But wait for a second, John, you're not going to get a perfect Master every time because all Brothers are different," I interjected. "Not all are going to do a great job as Master, but that doesn't mean that he should not have the opportunity."

"I agree, my Brother," he growled again impatiently. "But just because every American has the opportunity to be the President in our country doesn't mean that every person is qualified to do the job. I am saying that just like the job of President of the United States, our Fraternity and our Lodges are hurt badly by poor or weak leadership. And I am surely not saying that they are not good Masons. I am just saying that certain Brothers should not be allowed to run our Lodges just because he wants to. Any Brother who desires to be the Master of his Lodge if his motives are pure and he wants to further the aims and programs of his Lodge and the Grand Lodge and Masonry should be given the opportunity. However, there are too many of those Brothers out there whose only motivation to hold the office of Master is to have the honor of being known as a Past Master. They want all the privileges, prestige, and benefits that go with it. Those are the

Brothers that we cannot allow to become Master. Those Brothers do more damage to our Fraternity than almost anything."

"Are you saying that those Brothers want to hurt their Lodges?"

"No, I don't think that the harm and in some cases the destruction that they do to their Lodges is intentional. In many cases, I believe that they do not understand what is involved or realize the position's importance. Our normal system of advancing through the officers' positions, what we call 'moving up through the chairs,' allows the Lodge Brothers to gauge a Brother's commitment, energy, and, most importantly, leadership ability. We are our own worst enemies when it comes to selecting and advancing Brothers to officer positions in the Lodge. We elect them to a lower office, and we find out pretty quickly whether this Brother has what it takes to lead the Lodge. When we find out that a mistake has been made, we don't do anything about it.

It's crazy, Brother Chris. I have seen it many times. We don't have the intestinal fortitude to remove an obviously bad choice because we are afraid of hurting his feelings, losing him, or losing other Brothers. The end result is that he becomes Worshipful Master and severely harms and, in some cases, destroys his Lodge. Then the Lodge loses a lot more than a few Brothers. It loses the trust and goodwill of its members, losing the peace and harmony of the Lodge. Some Masons choose to attend a different Lodge or a different Masonic organization. It's just crazy that Masons don't understand the awesome responsibility and effect that the Master has on the Lodge. Being the Master of a Masonic Lodge is not a right. It is a privilege, an honor, and a reward for hard work, dedication, and commitment to the Lodge and Masonry. Those self-serving Brothers who seek to sit in the East for any other reason than to better their Lodge and serve their Brothers with honor and integrity need to be removed from the line-up and not allowed to continue."

Shaking my head, "Oh man, I would be afraid to be an officer in your Lodge. You are not going to tolerate anything but the best."

"Nooooo, that's not what I mean," John shot back. "A Brother does not have to be a professional manager or have a finance degree. Heck, he doesn't have to be a great speaker, but he *has* to have his Lodge and his Brothers' best interests foremost in his heart. He has to be a servant leader for them and not for himself. We don't have to have perfection, just true intentions. He needs to have a plan, and he needs to have the energy and the determination to make that plan happen. Brothers will follow a Brother who is true to himself and true to Masonry. The Brothers aren't looking for perfection, but they won't suffer laziness, indifference, or fraud. They will help a Brother who is busting his butt to get things done, but they won't lift a finger for one who talks a good game but won't put out the effort to do anything. Words mean nothing when they aren't followed by action."

"Heck, I'm with you, John. But how do we turn this around?"

"Unfortunately, it's a bigger problem than just voting a poor leader out of the line-up. It's poor leadership that causes the problem in the first place. A Lodge falls into a rut of not doing the work that a Lodge is supposed to do. They don't do any community or charitable work. They don't take care of their widows, orphans, or even their Brothers. They stop making Masons because they stop attracting good men. When they get a petitioner, they rush him through the process instead of following the proper procedure and doing a proper investigation. Then they rush him through his work without proper instruction or explanation. And when he finds out, and he will, that he has been shortchanged in his Masonic education, he will stop attending Lodge, go to another Lodge, or just quit altogether. And the blame for the failure always gets placed on the candidate not being ready to be a Mason instead of where it truly belongs, on the Lodge members themselves.

Someday, sometime maybe we will have a set of standards where a Lodge is required to maintain itself at a certain level of proficiency in all the things that a Lodge is supposed to do in order to be able to keep its Charter. If they don't, then that Lodge should be shut down and merged with another Lodge, or the officers should be replaced to get the Lodge back on the right track instead of allowing it to give Masonry and all Masons a bad name. I know I am rambling on Brother Chris, but I think this is a problem that needs to be addressed because it goes to one of our fundamental maxims in our Lodges which is peace and harmony."

I needed to get him calmed down a bit because people were starting to stare, so I reached over and grabbed his arms that he had been flailing about while he was talking and looked in his eyes and said slowly, "How about dessert?"

It was almost comical watching his mind trying to shift gears in mid-rant. John blinked a couple of times, and that goofy grin formed on his rather large round face, "If you insist."

After asking Shelly for a couple of thick slices of chocolate cake and of course, John had to have a couple of scoops of ice cream on the side. Boy, that sure did the trick on his attitude. Shelly laid the bill (diplomatically) equal distance between John and me, and he promptly slid it towards me. I glanced down at it and slid it over to John, who quickly slid it back to me. Shelly's eyes were following side to side back and forth, and after several passes across the table, she reached out and stopped it in mid pass, "I have seen everything now. I have seen people ignore the bill, I have seen people fight for the bill, but this is the first time I have seen a couple of guys trying to make the other one pay. You two don't look alike, but you act like you are Brothers."

Well, there we were, all three of us with a hand on the bill, John and I staring at each other. I don't know what he was thinking, but after she said that, it made me feel a little ashamed; I started to pull the bill back towards me and darned if John didn't start trying to do the same. Thirty seconds earlier, we were pushing it to the other guy, and now we were trying to take it back. Shelly saw what was happening and let out a sigh, and shook her head, "When you figure it, out call me." She turned and left us sitting there looking at each other.

Well, we both were trying to pay arguing back and forth until two ladies sitting next to us got up and left laughing and shaking their heads like we were crazy. Long story short, we finally got it figured out.... I paid.... what a surprise. When Shelly brought back my receipt, John informed her that we were in fact, Brothers and offered no further explanation. She just smiled and wished us a nice day. As I watched John drive off, I thought with a smile about what the word Brother means to all of us.

Yup, it means the world, doesn't it?

THE FOUR HORSEMEN AND THE NEED FOR CHANGE

I sure hope this doesn't come back to bite me in the you-know-what, but the Brothers and I were planning to do something a little crazy. I know it's a terrible way to start this story so let me get you caught up.

At Lodge earlier in the month, our Worshipful Master told me about a place he had gone to eat that he said had the hottest hamburger on the planet. It had a combination of several peppers and hot sauces on it altogether. The more he told me, the more I knew we had to take John there to eat. Patrick said that very few people have ever finished that burger, and many get physically sick. I didn't want to hurt Brother John at all but rather test his culinary constitution's outer limits. You would think that a guy that stands 6ft 7 inches tall and weighs in on a livestock scale at around 275 lbs. and eats like a proverbial horse would be able to get down any hamburger, no matter how hot it is. When the word got out what we wanted to do, everybody wanted to come. The next part was setting it up and coordinating everything to come together whenever John came through town. I always waited for John to call me each month as he passed through, but this time I needed time to prepare, so I made the call.

John was a little surprised to hear from me since I never call him. I told him I had a special place to take him to eat this month and needed to make sure we could go when he was in town. Of course, John was excited and gave me the date he was coming. I must admit to you *on the square* that I failed to tell him everything about where we were going.

As it turned out, I only had to wait a couple of days. On the prescribed day and time, John showed up at the shop, raring to go. I loaded him up (in the case he couldn't drive afterward), and off we went. I asked for a special dispensation from Leonard for a long lunch. I had heard this might take a while.

It was about a 25-minute drive. When we pulled up at the Chunky Hamburgers' parking lot, I noticed several of my Lodge Brothers' cars already parked there. I told John that some of the Brothers were also coming, and he was excited to see them again. In the process of parking my truck, unloading John, and walking across the parking lot, I told John that this was going to be the spiciest, hottest burger he ever ate. I followed up by stating that very few people have ever finished it.

"Brother Chris, they ain't never made anything spicy that could bother this old boy."

I shook my head, "But John, this thing has three different kinds of peppers on it. It has jalapenos, serrano peppers, and some kind of pepper called Naga Jolokia. *Heck, they call it the Ghost Pepper!* It's the hottest pepper known to man, it sounds a little scary to me. Then they pour habanero chili sauce all over it. It's so hot that you have to sign a waiver before they will let you eat it."

John tossed back at me. "Pshhhh, A waiver, you say? I'm thinking it's a lot of build-up to a big let-down. Show me this so-called spicy hot burger." I just shrugged and opened the door for him.

The Brothers were all there waiting for him. John had a surprised look on his face as he greeted them one by one. We led him over to the table, and April, our server, came over to take our orders. I announced to her that my friend and Brother Big John Deacon was here to take on the *Four Horsemen Burger.*

April got a solemn look on her face, "You do know what that means, don't you." Well, we all nodded except John, who was looking around the table a little confused.

"I'll be right back," April said and disappeared into the kitchen. Pretty quick, she was back with a paper and pen in her hand which she sat down in front of John. "You have to fill this out before the cook will make a *Four Horsemen Burger."*

John just looked at her and shook his head like we were all crazy and picked up the pen and the paper.

There was a place to print his name right after the letter **I** and just before **being of sound mind and not being inebriated in any way**, which John thought was a little amusing. The second question concerned **not being pregnant and never being able to be**. Then John had to **promise not to get sick and make a mess all over the place**.

While John was mulling over the questions, April told him that it would cost 20.00, but if he finished the *Four Horseman Burger* in under 25 minutes, it would be free. That made John's day.

"Well, Miss April Flowers, looks like this boy is eating free today." I don't think her last name was Flowers. I don't know where he got that.

April just smiled a knowing smile and pointed at the paper. John finally finished filling out the disclaimer, much to the delight of all the Brothers around the table. A loud cheer went up when April called out towards the kitchen, *"We got a sucker out here who says he can eat a Four*

Horsemen!" April made a gesture towards John, "and this fine Gentleman says he wants one also." We got a big laugh out of that; meanwhile, John looked around for the *sucker*. He had a confused look on his face.

The rest of us ordered several trays of their awesome chili cheese tots to snack on while we waited for John's burger. Boy, this was going to be good. April returned with a galvanized bucket like we used to feed horses out of on the ranch. She set it down next to John, who looked up with a puzzled expression on his face.

"That's for when you get sick, big boy," April said matter-of-factly and then disappeared again.

John looked over at me, grinned, "That little filly don't know who she is dealing with."

In a matter of minutes, April appeared at the table with the *Four Horsemen Burger,* and I swear I could see what looked like fumes rising off of it. She sat it down in front of John, who immediately saw it was just a regular-sized burger and looked up at April, "Darlin, if I had known it was this small, I would have ordered three. You'd better get another couple of these started real quick."

I caught her eye and shook my head, but she was way ahead of me. "Big John, honey, If you eat that burger in front of you, I promise that you are going to need a nap before you eat another, but I will put the kitchen on standby just in case."

With that, she handed John a pair of latex gloves and told him to wear them to handle the burger so he wouldn't burn his hands or eyes if he were to rub them later on and possibly be blinded. I heard John mumble something, which I couldn't wholly hear about his mother telling him about rubbing and being blinded as he stretched the gloves over his massive paws. As John reached down and picked his burger up, I whispered in his ear that he might want to take a small bite to start. John just gave me a sideways glance of irritation and took a big bite. I heard a sharp intake of breath from a few of the onlookers. We watched as John took a couple of chews and stopped. Then he took another couple of chews with no expression on his face. John just looked straight ahead.

We were all amazed. I thought for sure John would be hurting by now. We waited as he chewed some more (still the first bite). The first sign of trouble was when I noticed tears starting to pour out of both of his eyes. Out of the corner of my eye, I thought I saw money changing hands. Apparently, the smart money was on Big John. He finally swallowed that first bite, followed by a massive cheer from the Brothers and other diners gathered around the table. Then John slowly leaned over towards me like he wanted to say something. I leaned over to him. His breath burned my ear as he whispered for me to cancel the other two burgers he ordered. I just nodded, and without any expression, he took his second bite, which was a bit smaller than the first. Slowly John chewed that bite and then another, and finally, he got both down. The tears were rolling out by now, and his face had turned a bright shade of pink. Again, John slowly leaned over towards me. This time I shielded my ear as he spoke. In a hoarse whisper, I could barely understand, "Brother Chris, I can't feel my tongue. Can you see if it's still there?"

I looked, "John, your tongue is still there. How do you feel big guy? Ready to call it quits yet?"

With a painful smile on his face, John straightened up, "I feel just peachy."

John got through the subsequent two small bites, which brought him to about half the burger eaten. He paused again. By now, both eyes were very red, and John was breathing a little fast. I was starting to think that bringing him here was a mistake. I don't mean I shouldn't have had him eat here; I mean I shouldn't have let him ride with me. It could be a problem later on, but it was a little late to start thinking about that.

I looked up at the clock and saw that he had only 15 minutes left to finish or I was going to be out $20.00. I leaned in and told him he had 15 minutes to finish the burger. John looked at me and made a face that I took for a smile and nodded. He then slid the bucket over to me and motioned for me to fill it up with a drink.

April was watching everything and said quickly, "Nothing to drink. If you drink, you will be disqualified."

John stared at April for a few seconds and then straight ahead. Someone on the other side of the long table started chanting John…. John …. slowly at first, and others joined in. The cadence picked up, and they chanted faster and faster until every person in the room had joined in; *John! John! John! John!*

Suddenly John got a giant smile on his face and let out a huge roar. In three bites, he had finished off the *Four Horsemen Burger*. The chant turned to cheers as John chewed fast and hard. I hoped he could swallow and not explode after he did. John chewed for about 30 seconds and swallowed hard. The crowd went crazy cheering and clapping, and right at that moment is when I got into trouble with John.

He reached for my drink to extinguish the fire in his mouth and belly. I grabbed it away and told him he couldn't have anything to drink for five minutes after he finished. John got a look of horror on his face as he stared at me. His look changed to irritation and then to anger as he reached for my neck.

"*John!* It's just five minutes. You already ate it in plenty of time. Just hold on."

He sat there and glared at me until the five minutes were up. April grabbed his hand like a prized fighter and raised it. I slid the bucket over to him as he downed the last of his drink, thinking it was all about to come right back out. Much to everyone's amusement, John pushed the bucket away and reached for the basket of chili cheese tots in the middle of the table and started eating them. I glanced at the clock and realized I had overstayed my lunch dispensation, and I needed to get back to work. John said he was ready to leave too. We said goodbye to everyone, and John got a hug from April; he always gets the hugs. We headed for my truck. When we got to the truck, I could tell John was moving kinda slow. I leaned him up against the door and went back in and purchased one of those galvanized buckets; just in case.

I got him into the truck. John immediately reclined his seat and announced he needed to go straight to his hotel room instead of going all the way back to the shop. I complied and drove straight there.

John was moving slower and slower. As he walked, he declared that he wanted to go to sleep. I helped him to his room. As he sat on the edge of the bed, John realized that we hadn't talked about the newsletter yet. I told him it was OK. John said that he had something he wanted to say, so I sat down on the other bed and waited. After about a minute and a half, he looked up, "I am so tired, Brother Chris."

"I know, John. I am going to let you sleep. I need to get back to work before I lose my job."

"No, no, that's not what I am talking about. I am just so tired of seeing our Fraternity die a slow death. We cannot survive without new members. We act like we think we can. It's a selfish attitude to have. Masonry is to be shared and offered to all good men, but we seem to do everything possible to keep that from happening. Let me stop and explain. Every time a discussion like this comes up, certain narrow-minded Brothers jump on their bandwagons. They put their fingers in their ears and proceed to vilify the Brother by accusing him of wanting to destroy our Fraternity. Because the Brother mentions bringing in men who don't qualify to be members by our rules and standards. Or he wants new Brothers to shortcut the ritual or, worse yet, do away with the work altogether or at least change the work. He gets accused of turning the Craft into some diluted form of its original intent and purpose. But none of that is true. I don't know of anyone who wants to do any of that.

We gotta stop living in the past, Brother Chris. We need to start living in the present with our eyes forward-looking to the future. Sure, the past was an easier time, and it sure feels good to go back there in our minds and relive the good times, but the world changes. People change, attitudes change, and ideas change. I see it all the time. Older Brothers want to run the Lodges just like we did 30, 40, or 50 years ago. I sure wish we could do that, but we cannot. It won't work, and it is not working. Here we are, trying to attract new members without understanding how men in their 20's and 30's think and make no effort to try to understand. I keep hearing that these youngsters want to change Masonry and make it into something unrecognizable. Most of the ones saying this are so pig-headed in their opinions and attitudes that they won't even consider that their views are not based on facts.

The sad truth is that our Fraternity does not appeal to the younger generations. We refuse to change with the times with respect to how we run our Lodges. We sit around and whine and moan about how long it's been since we got any new members, but everything we do is designed to keep young men from joining. It doesn't mean that young men who are told about what Masons stand for don't want to be Masons because they do. They believe in who we are and what we do, but when they see how we run our Lodges and how outdated our views are, joining a Lodge is not appealing.

Why can't we get it through our heads that Masonry is and always will be attractive to all men regardless of age, in its original form with all its old charges and tenets, with all its ancient rituals and obligations intact? We have the product, Masonry, but we have gotten old. Old in our minds, old in our thinking, old in our attitudes, and old in our buildings. We have failed to do our maintenance. We have lived on the memories of long ago when Masonry was booming.

Now other organizations whose only purpose is charitable activity get the good men that we should be getting. We offer more than charity. We provide unequaled wealth in the moral and spiritual development of men's minds and souls. I realize that statement will probably irritate a few Brothers, but Brethren, who know me, know what I mean. Those younger men that we so desperately need to keep our Fraternity growing aren't going to come to the same old pancake breakfast every year. They are not going to get their wives to go to our old and severely under-maintained buildings. The Brothers always say we don't have the money to fix our buildings. Of course, we don't. We handle our finances in the past also, and now it has come back to bite us. We have to raise our dues in big jumps because we haven't kept pace economically with the changing times. Guess who is threatening to quit the Fraternity because the dues need to be raised to save our Grand Lodge and our Lodges? Yup, the same Brothers who want us to live in the past, the same Brothers who are blind to what is staring them right in the face. They threaten to quit. What kind of Brothers are they? Is it possible that Masonry doesn't have the meaning to them that it should? Maybe we have already become that social club we are afraid of becoming. We can't seem to separate ancient charges and rituals from outdated thinking. The world changes, and we don't or won't change with it.

How low will we have to sink before we realize we made a wrong turn a long time ago. When are enough Masons going to recognize that our ancient Craft and work can coexist with modern administration and ideas without harming or changing what has survived centuries? Are we going to have to lose this precious Brotherhood entirely and leave it to future generations to try to raise it from the ashes of obscurity? Is this what we want? You cannot solve today's problems with solutions from the past."

"Whew, John, you said a lot right there. Are you OK?"

"Yeah, I'm OK." he responded, a little out of breath. "Just tired, and ohhhh, a little queasy in the stomach. Are you going to put all that in your newsletter?"

"I sure am. Why?"

"Well, you are going to find out who reads this column," John snickered. "You are going to hear from every Brother who agrees and also every Brother who disagrees. Hope you have some thick skin."

"Well, it is what it is, John. I want to tell you about my thoughts on..." I looked over, and right in the middle of my sentence, John was snoring. I guess the day was pretty traumatic for him. But John did it. He conquered the *Four Horsemen Burger*. I let myself out. Me and my bucket headed back to the shop. I had a couple of questions for him, but they will have to wait till tomorrow when I bring him his truck.

THE MOST IMPORTANT MEAL OF THE DAY AND THE DUTIES OF A PAST MASTER

Well, it almost happened again. You know how in Vegas that if you win big or catch you counting cards or cheating, they won't let you come back to that casino? They ban you for life. That's what almost happened to me. No, I didn't get caught cheating at cards, I haven't won big at anything, and it's not in Vegas either. What I am referring to is right here in town. Over the last few months, I thought that John had mellowed out a bit, but of course, I was wrong. My Brother, A-La-Humongous, Big John Deacon almost managed to get me, and himself, of course, banned from all of the Jim's Restaurants. That would have been really sad because they have the best chicken fried steak and eggs plate in town. When you slap some of their excellent hash brown potatoes on the side, you've got an almost heavenly breakfast. You can probably tell that I go there a lot, or I should say, I used to go there a lot.

John called and said he couldn't stop by this month but would be passing through town early in the morning on his way to a sales meeting. I agreed to meet him for breakfast, and he suggested one of my favorites; Jim's Restaurant. John was walking in the front door as I pulled up and parked. Since it was just 6 AM, there weren't very many diners there yet, but I knew it would fill up fast in the next hour. John found a spot at one of the several stools at the bar by the time I got inside. He was already perusing the menu with a smile on his face.

"Brother Chris, you know that breakfast is the most important meal of the day. And you know that I am still a growing boy. I must start off the day with a proper nutritious breakfast."

"Yup, I do know you are a growing boy. It's where you are growing that is the concern. When is the last time you got a checkup from a doctor?"

John gave me the evil eye over the top of his menu, "If I don't get my three-square meals a day and at least two snacks, I get real grouchy."

"OK, OK, I hear you," as I waved the waitress over.

Her name was Shirley, and she had red hair, bright red lipstick, and a great smile. John looked up at her over his menu, "Darlin, how good is that cook of yours in making a big plate of Huevos Rancheros?"

"Well, Sugar, no one has complained yet. So, I'd day pretty good."

"Well then, Darlin, better tell him to rustle me up a double order."

"Ok, Sugar," she purred with her cute Texas accent. "Coming right up." And with that, she turned toward the kitchen.

I cleared my throat loudly, and she turned back with a quizzical look on her face. "I hate to break in on the Darlin, Sugar thing y'all got going on, but can I order too?"

She was a little embarrassed, "Oh my gosh, what can I get you?" (notice I didn't get a Darlin, Sugar, or anything)

I ordered my usual chicken fried steak and eggs and sat back to soak in any wisdom that John might have to give out. The only thing John really had to say was that it took him almost four days to heal up from the Four Horsemen Burger he had when we met last month, but he was glad he had eaten it anyway. We could see the cook working on our orders through the opening between the back counter and the kitchen. Pretty soon, the cook sat John's plate, which was more of a platter, up on the counter followed closely by mine and shouted out to Shirley. She grabbed them both and did a 180 to set them in front of us. John dug right in, and in no time flat, he had half of the plate gone.

The cook had been watching and called out to John, "Hey Buddy, how're those huevos rancheros?"

"They are pretty darn good Pardner, but I think the ones I make at home are better."

Well, that's when it started. The cook challenged John to come back in the kitchen and prove that his huevos rancheros were better. Danged if John didn't (over my objections) get up and head into the kitchen. I just knew this wasn't going to end well. I saw the cook's name was Tony. Tony handed John an apron, and I could hear them talking back and forth as he showed John where everything was located. I munched on my steak and eggs, amused, but I didn't have a real good feeling about this. It couldn't have been more than 10 minutes when Tony and John emerged from the kitchen with two big platters of food. They took away my plate, which irritated me because I wasn't done yet. Then they sat the two platters in front of me and demanded that I try both and tell them which was better. I just shrugged and tasted the one that Tony had made, and it was delicious. The ranchero sauce was tangy and was paired perfectly with the bell peppers and onions in the eggs. Tony crossed his arms and smiled at John after hearing what I had to say. I then looked at what John had made, and I have to say it looked fantastic. He had made the scrambled eggs with a little more bell peppers and onions than Tony's. John sprinkled a little shredded sharp cheddar cheese and heaped two big spoonful's of fresh pico de gallo on top. I tasted it, and while I was chewing, my mind was racing, trying to figure out what to say to not hurt Tony's feelings too much cause John's pico eggs were fantastic. They were staring at me pretty hard, and I knew I had to be careful. I took another bite which didn't sit well with Tony.

I really liked John's eggs better, but I wanted to keep the peace. I thought for a second longer what to say that would cause the least amount of harm. "I can't really tell which one is the best. They are both delicious."

Well, instead of that making things better, they got a whole lot worse real quick. John and Tony looked at me and then at each other and started arguing about why their dish was better. Both started waving other customers up to the counter to try the two platters. I literally got pushed out of the way, but I managed to reach and grab my original plate before retreating to a nearby table to watch the show. So much for keeping the peace. Several diners came up to the counter at the beckoning of John and Tony. The two platters of food were gone in no time, and they both told everyone to hold fast. They disappeared back to the kitchen to make more dishes. They were soon back, and the waiting (and hungry) diners dug right into the new plates. Both John and Tony had outdone themselves. The food was great, and a consensus as to which was better never came about. Everyone agreed that it was all good. Happy with all of their appetites satisfied, everyone started leaving one by one.

I began to think that I was worrying for nothing until it hit me as the manager came in the front door and saw all the diners leaving without paying for anything. The look on his face was not pretty at all. It was a cross between shock, surprise, and anger. The manager looked from face to face to face as people happily walked through the doors to their cars. His gaze then slowly swung around to the two big guys in aprons, one employed by the restaurant and the other one that to the best of his knowledge was not. They were standing behind the counter, trying to look invisible as they realized that in their zealous pursuit of who could cook the best breakfast, they had fed everyone in the restaurant ......for *FREE.*

Both had the guilty look of a dog as he realizes you are supremely mad at him because you came home from work and discovered that he has destroyed the trash and everything not tied down while you were gone. Everyone, the manager, John, Tony, Shirley, and yup, even me, stayed real still looking around from person to person like in the movie High Noon just before all the shooting started. The manager's gaze finally settled on me, and I quickly took out my wallet, showed him, and pointed to my plate. He said nothing and turned back to John and Tony, who looked really small considering how big they were. The manager walked up to John and asked him to please sit with me while he talked to Tony. As they disappeared into the kitchen, I saw that customers had been filing in, and things had returned pretty much to normal. I looked over at John. He was real quiet.

"I don't know what you are laughing at. I am in real trouble here Brother. Don't you see that?"

I looked at John in disbelief and, trying hard not to laugh, "Brother John, you don't work here. He can't fire you."

"Yeah, but he is really mad. Didn't you see the look on his face? He looked like he was about to blow a gasket."

"Yup, he sure is, but the guy you need to be worried about is Tony. He might get fired. Ultimately, what happened here just now was initiated by him. Technically you didn't ask to have a cooking contest."

That bothered John, and I could see that he was worried about Tony. To get his mind off the situation, I asked John to give me something I could pass along to all the Brethren reading the newsletter. John tried to make me promise not to say anything about this fiasco, but like my nieces both tell me all the time, yeah, right! He kept glancing towards the kitchen and then back at me. I told him to concentrate.

In a few seconds, John's expression changed as he focused, shaking his head slowly, "Brother Chris, I am always getting distressed over things that I see that just don't seem right. I see Brothers who finish their time in the East, served on a Grand Lodge Committee, or even the presiding officer of another Masonic organization, and somehow, they conclude that they have done their time. They just lay down their tools and stop working. They stop teaching, stop learning, and they stop growing. Pretty soon, they stop caring. I just can't hardly understand it. When I see this, I wonder if Masonry has failed them, but then I quickly realize that Masonry cannot fail anyone. It is pure truth and goodness. It never stops giving. It never stops teaching or revealing. Like a familiar old blanket, it is always warm and comforting. How can they just stop?"

"I don't know, John. Do you think it could be because they just get tired? There are so many things that might contribute to them being tired."

John looked at me thoughtfully for a few seconds and slowly nodded, "I think you are right, Brother Chris but maybe not in the way you are thinking. When you get tired or worn out, you just rest and begin your work again. I think these Brothers get tired in another way. These Masons have learned, studied, and worked hard teaching new Masons. They have put in the time and effort to be true students of the Craft. Still, beyond the mandatory requirements of learning, there is little interest in pursuing a path of Masonic enlightenment. This is a disturbingly large percentage of Brothers. Take a look around, and you will see fewer and fewer Brothers who want to study and learn. There are fewer and fewer who care to read about the most basic things about the Craft. It just doesn't seem to be that important to them. It sometimes seems that our philanthropic works have become more important than the moral and spiritual path that Masonry sets out for us to follow. Certainly, the Fraternity's principles and tenets go hand in hand with being charitable, but charity was not meant to be the primary duty of Masonry.

Seeing all this happening around the Craft I think these learned Brothers just don't think there is a reason to teach anymore, and they just stop. But just because there are Brothers who won't read or study, we *CAN* still teach. We *CAN* still present Masonic programs on education, philosophy, ritual, and yes, even charity in our Lodges. We need these wise Brethren to pass along the experience and wisdom of Lodge administration and communication that they have obtained over their years of dedicated service to the Craft. We cannot let these Brothers think that they are not needed. We cannot let them put themselves out to pasture.

Brothers tell me that they hate to read but enjoy getting Masonic education from other Brothers who present programs at their meetings. Over the years, I have been to many Lodges. I have seen almost no Masonic education going on during meetings. No one is teaching. But I know that Brothers are sitting in the chairs on the sidelines who could be effective teachers and lecturers in the different areas of Masonry. Just because a Brother doesn't like to read doesn't mean he doesn't want to learn or won't learn. Heck, when I was a kid, I hated broccoli, but my mother always put it on the table and tried to get me to eat it. I tried it but absolutely didn't like it. Now I am older, and guess what? I love broccoli! I could eat it all the time. The point is that we have to keep working at dispensing Masonic education because people change. The Ritual is amazing, and it dispenses much information, but it only goes so far. There is much more to learn and much more to experience."

"I agree, John, but how do we get more Brothers to get interested in education beyond the mandatory ritualistic instruction?"

"*We don't just get them to; we do like mom did.* We put it on the table and allow them to try it, and when they finally do, some of them are gonna like it. We just can't stop putting it on the table."

Before I could tell him, I agreed with him completely, the kitchen door swung open, and the manager came over to us. Talk about putting it on the table; I knew this would be something we weren't going to like. As he was walking toward us, I noticed that Tony was back at the stove cooking up a storm, so I guess he didn't get fired after all. That was good. The manager had a stern look on his face and held out his hand to me. He introduced himself as Roland. I shook his hand and told him my name but kinda stuttered in the middle of it when I felt a real familiar grip. I looked up, and he gave me a little wink. I grinned as he turned to John and fixed him with a stern look. John looked mighty apologetic as Roland began to talk. He told John that Tony had taken all the responsibility for everything. John said to him that it was his fault and that Tony was not guilty of anything.

"I thought you might say that, so here is what I propose we do. Tony told me that your pico eggs were pretty darn good, so I propose that in exchange for us losing all that business this morning, you give us the recipe for your dish for free, so we can use it. Secondly, I need you to work in the kitchen for the next two hours to train Tony and my other cooks on making it. Does that sound fair?"

John chirped out happily, "*Well, Gol durn, that sounds like a deal to me!* I am glad Tony is not in trouble."

"Good, now let's go to work. I lost a lot of business because of you two, and I got to make up the difference somehow."

Roland turned to me, shook my hand again, "Brother Chris, it was nice to meet you. Brother John and I have to go to work now." I just smiled and nodded as he turned and walked back to the kitchen.

You should have seen the look on John's face. He looked at me and then at Roland and kinda stuttered a couple of times, but no real words came out. I just smiled and waved as John turned towards the kitchen, calling out to Roland to wait. I paid my bill and thanked the Supreme Architect of the Universe for not having to pay for John this month, or all for those patrons that walked out the door. John was hootin and hollerin and having a fine time in the kitchen as I walked out the door. It's gonna be a great month…. I can feel it.

It's All About the Forks and Laughter Really is the Best Medicine

Brother Anthony, a good friend from another Lodge, gave me some tickets to the local Comedy Club. A friend of his was scheduled to perform. The friend performing is a hypnotist. Pam and I met several of my Lodge Brothers there. As usual, I was alternately checking my watch and asking Pam when she would be ready when the doorbell rang. Thinking it must be one of my neighbors, I opened the door. To my surprise, my expansive Brother John Deacon was standing there. "What the heck are you doing here, John? Why didn't you call?"

"I was driving through on my way back home and not feeling good about driving another five hours. I decided to see if you were home. It was just a last-minute decision. Looks like you and the Misses are going out, so I will just catch you another time."

Well, what could I do? "Come on in, John, you are going out to the Comedy Club with us."

John mumbled something about not intruding on our evening as he shouldered his way past me to give Pam a hug. Actually, it worked out pretty good because she kinda brightened up and seemed to forget the last half hour of my pressuring her to get ready. As usual, I had to drive faster than I had intended to get there. John complained all the way downtown about how hungry he was. I told him we were late and that they had food at the club; at least, I sure hoped they did. We got there in time. After shaking hands with the other Brothers of my Lodge, Brother Anthony took us to the seats he had saved for all of us, right up next to the stage.

Sure enough, there was a menu on the table. John grabbed it and waved at the server at the same time. I wasn't paying attention to him, but soon she was sitting all kinds of stuff on the table in front of John. There were jalapeno poppers and cheese fries with chili, of course, cheese sticks and chips and queso with a side of salsa. I noticed a couple of plates that had something on them that I could not identify in the club's low light. You know, all the healthy stuff. *Yuck!!!* I made a mental note to ask Brother Brad to take John back to his hotel after the show because by the looks of the things John was consuming, it might be a rather aromatic trip home.

Right then, the show started. The hypnotist came out and explained to everyone what he was going to do. He said that those who volunteered to be hypnotized for the two-hour show would benefit from about ten hours of excellent sleep. He invited anyone who wanted to be part of the show to come up on stage. I felt something brush by me and looked up to see John heading for the stage. I reached out, stopped him, and asked him if he was sure he wanted to go up there since he would probably be told to do some really off-the-wall stuff.

"Brother Chris, I haven't had a lick of sleep in two days, and I sure need it. Surely it can't be that bad."

With that, John headed for the stage. What happened, no one could have predicted. I saw that Monica, one of the ladies from our group, had gone to the stage and Brother Brad, his wife, Crystal and Brother Jason. During the process of putting everyone to sleep, Gary, the hypnotist, saw that Brad had a sly grin on his face and wasn't responding to the suggestions to fall asleep, so he pulled him up and sent him back to our table. In no time at all, Gary had the rest of them fast asleep and leaning on one another. That's when the fun started. I haven't laughed so much in a long time. Over the next hour, Gary had them watching Leprechauns running under their chairs and singing crazy songs. He told them that the person sitting next to them had passed gas, and they were all giving each other mean looks and holding their noses. Then he told them all that they were driving, and to grab the wheel. While all nine of them were casually driving their cars, he told them that they had driven into a nudist colony, and there were a bunch of naked people on their right. Of course, the guys were looking. The girls were peeking, except one held up her hand to the side of her face and refused to look. But John just about fell off his chair, looking all around. If he had been really driving, he would have crashed for sure. Whatever he saw, it was clear that he liked it. Me and everyone else in the audience were almost falling off our chairs, laughing at him.

Gary then had all of them thinking that someone in the audience had the hots for them, so they were smiling and winking. They were all trying to attract whomever it was in the audience they thought was looking at them. Then he told all of them that the person next to them was thinking inappropriate thoughts about them. That was pretty funny because all the girls were clearly upset and disgusted, but all the guys were smiling and happy except John, the only guy sitting next to another guy. He was not happy at all.

When I thought I couldn't laugh anymore, each of them was given a specific task to perform when a certain word was said. All were pretty hilarious, but when Gary told John that he was a male dancer at a bachelorette party for the ladies at the table in front of the stage, Brother Brad and I just about lost it. John's music came on; he jumped up and immediately pulled off his shirt. Watching my 275-pound Brother jiggle and gyrate shirtless across the stage towards the ladies' table, it was hard to decide whether to laugh or cry. The ladies at the table were senior citizens for sure and were hootin and cackling up a storm. John danced (I guess you could call it dancing) over to their table and was gyrating his hips (Boy, was he going to be sore the next day), and those ladies were loving it. Then he did something only John would do. As he was bent over the ladies' table just dancing his rear end off, John caught sight of a cheese stick sitting all by its lonesome on a plate. In the blink of an eye, he grabbed it in his teeth and danced around the table, chewing on that cheese stick. While I was shaking my head a little embarrassed, the ladies and the rest of the audience were eating it up.... John's performance that is.

Mercifully, Gary finally went over and steered John back to his seat and made him put his shirt back on. With everyone pretty much laughing out loud, he gave them some post-hypnotic suggestions. Gary told them that they would remember everything that happened, and they would feel like they had 10 hours of sleep. Then he woke them all up, and the participants returned to their tables, all insisting that they had not been hypnotized.... including John. Gary thanked all the volunteers and told John not to give up his day job. Gary recognized the Masons and Shriners in the audience and recognized all the good they do.

As we were leaving, I realized that John hadn't said anything in the last three hours that any of my readers would want to hear, and of course, he soon started complaining that he was hungry. John seemed puzzled since he had just had 5 plates of food ....and one extra cheese stick. I reminded him that he had just done a complete aerobic workout and worked off what he already ate. I said my goodbyes to the group and loaded Mr. Chippendale up to head for home. We had to drive through a Whataburger so John could get a triple cheeseburger. I didn't even know that they made a *triple*.

John ate in silence as we drove, and when he was done, I looked back at him, "Well?"

"Well, what?"

"This is our only meeting this month, and I have readers that are out there hanging onto your every word."

John looked at me like I was nuts. Finally, he sat back and took a deep breath, "Brother Chris, I want to talk about the forks."

"Oh my gosh, John, are you still hungry? I am asking for some profound Masonic wisdom, and you are fantasizing about eating utensils."

John gave me a long sad look like he felt sorry for my lack of intelligence, slowly shook his head, "My poor, poor, Brother Chris, do you believe that I only think about food…. now cut that out (as he saw me nodding my head) and let me finish. I am talking about the forks in the road that the Great Architect of the Universe leads us to every day."

John saw the puzzled look on my face, "Don't change the channel on me, Brother. Hang in there a little bit while I explain." John's voice got real serious, "Brother Chris, have you ever made a mistake?" Before I could answer, Pam let out her breath a little too strongly and shook her head, which didn't make me look that good.

"Are you kidding, John?" as I glanced sideways at Pam. "I have made some doozies. Some I am not very proud of."

"And have you ever made a mistake that was so bad that you thought that everyone would give up on you, or you felt so bad that you thought you would never be able to make it right?"

"Yup, I've been there before," I told him in a low voice. John smiled a knowing smile, Me too, Brother, me too. But you know that we come to a fork in the road every day and often have to make a decision. For example, the store's cashier gives us too much change or the person next to your car drops his wallet on the ground. Maybe the person at the drive-through gave you an extra burger. These are all tests…. forks in the road."

I interrupted, "I don't see you giving back an extra burger, but I think I know what you mean."

"As I said," John growled, giving me the evil eye. "These are forks in the road to see if you will make the right decision or the wrong one. And you know what, we always know before, what the right decision is but we still sometimes make the wrong decision or do the wrong thing. When we do, we fall. The big guy grabs our hand and picks us up and leads us back to that fork in the road and gives us another chance to do the right thing."

"The big guy???"

John gave me a stern look and pointed skyward, "Yup, he never gives up on us. No matter how many times we make the wrong decision. We always have another chance to learn the lesson he is trying to get us to understand. If we keep fighting it and taking the wrong fork, again and again, he will lead us back to the fork and give us another chance. Some people never learn and keep falling and falling their whole life but most finally figure it out. Did you ever see that movie *Bull Durham?"*

Without waiting for my answer, he went on, "Well, this old catcher in the minor leagues was assigned to teach a rookie pitcher the ropes so he could move up to the majors. This rookie pitcher wanted to do things his way and throw whatever pitch he wanted when he wanted, and he just couldn't manage to get the hitters to strike out but still kept making those wrong decisions. Every time the pitcher would refuse to throw what the catcher asked for, he would tell the hitter what the pitch was, and of course, the hitter would hit the heck out of it.... usually a home run. Finally, the pitcher figured it out and decided to throw exactly what the catcher called for, and all of a sudden, things got a lot better, and soon he went up to the Major Leagues. The pitcher decided to start making the right decisions. He could have made that decision a lot earlier and saved himself a lot of time, but in the grand scheme of things, the point is every time you come to a fork in the road, you should make the right decision without even thinking about it.

It's kinda like our Masonry. We Masons follow the Great Architect of the Universe's rule and guide, and Brothers always support one another, helping them in all their distresses. That support system of Brothers who teach and learn by the good example and good counsel of other Brothers leads us to that ultimate goal of always making the right decision. Doing the right thing without having to think about it first. While we enjoy the benefits that doing the right thing provides, suddenly, here comes another fork in the road and another chance to do the right thing. It's all about the forks Brother Chris. He (again pointing up) will always give you the opportunity to do the right thing, but the final decision is yours and mine alone. It always has been and always will be. Yes, when everyone else gives up on you, and even when you give up on yourself, the Great Architect of the Universe never gives up on you. I have come to look forward to those forks in the road, Brother Chris. I enjoy having the opportunity to do the right thing. The more I do, the better I feel about everything."

"Brother John, I really enjoyed what you said, and I will enjoy bringing your message to all the Brethren. Thanks for the lesson. Instead of going to a hotel, why don't you just sleep on our couch tonight?"

"Thanks for the offer, but other than feeling a little sore, which I can't figure out, I feel great and wide awake. I am going to drive on home tonight."

Pam and I tried to talk him into staying, but he shook my hand and gave Pam a hug. He climbed into that big truck of his and headed for home. It was a good night and a good lesson. Later just before I nodded off to sleep, it came to me how much I have grown as a man and a Mason since I have known Big John Deacon. Despite all of the frustration he causes me and the trouble he gets into, I like him a lot.

God Bless You, Brother John.

SHRIMP, SHRIMP, AND MORE SHRIMP AND DON'T CHANGE THE PENALTIES

I almost didn't have a John Deacon article this month. If the truth be known, I was exhausted and not really looking forward to the monthly visit by his highness and wideness. However, I have learned two things; Brother John will not be denied and he will seldom pick up the check for lunch. I went back not long ago and tried to figure up how much I have spent feeding him over the past four years. I realized that I could have paid for two cruise vacations and a trip to see Pam's sisters in Oklahoma, a revelation that I will not be sharing with her. I would appreciate you keeping this on the square.

Anyway, John called, and I let it ring several times before taking a deep breath and answering it. I didn't even get a chance to say hello before he started talking.

"Brother Chris, what took you so long to answer?" Without waiting for my reply, "I have a lot to tell you, but I can't do it on an empty stomach. Where are you taking me to eat?"

John couldn't see me rolling my eyes, "Where would you like to go that both of us can eat for under ten dollars?"

"Hey, that's pretty funny, pard!" He was laughing, not taking the hint. "I was thinking about Seafood."

"*What do you mean, Seafood?* You mean like, when you see food, you eat it?"

John growled back, "You know what, I have told you many times before that you are not funny. I am almost at your place, and you haven't decided on what we are eating. I like shrimp a whole lot."

"You mean you like a whole lot of shrimp," I shot back to a dead phone. John had already hung up. Soon I looked up to see him standing in the doorway with his hands on his hips, and a look that communicated, *why are we not on our way?*

Well, John said shrimp, so I headed for the best shrimp I know; at Sea Island Shrimp House. On the way there, I made the mistake of asking how John had been doing since I saw him last month. He got a woebegone look on his face and told me that he had been asked to protem as Secretary at his Lodge's stated meeting the week before. The Lodge had just updated its sound system, and it was the first meeting using it.

The Junior Warden had clandestinely planted a flatulence machine under the Secretary's desk, and every time John started to speak, a sound which resembled an extreme passing of gas would emanate from the Secretary's desk followed by laughter from the Brethren. This went on throughout his reading of the minutes. He knew that he hadn't made the sounds and thought they had come from a malfunctioning microphone, so John continued with his reading and reporting. Much to the Brothers' delight, the sounds continued, and John moved the mic around to different spots until he finally turned it off. The sounds didn't stop, so John turned off the computer used to type the minutes; still, with no success, to stop the fart noises. Not knowing the true source of the sounds, John began to think they were accidental. So, he began to have fun with it and fanned the air behind him when he got up to have the Worshipful Master sign the minutes. After the meeting, the Brothers finally told him, and everyone had a big laugh. John claimed he was traumatized by it all, but I think he enjoyed it.

We got to Sea Island Shrimp House, and I watched as John ordered about every kind of shrimp they had. He had equal portions of fried shrimp, shrimp scampi, coconut shrimp, grilled shrimp, shrimp gumbo, and another type of shrimp I could not identify. John topped it off with French fries that four ordinary people could eat. I got a regular plate of popcorn shrimp and fries. I watched as the girl put four cocktail sauce containers on our tray with some ketchup. John asked for some tartar sauce and more cocktail sauce. She put one more of each. John cocked his head and gave her a questioning look, so she added one more of each which made him raise his eyebrows, coercing her into two more of each. Finally, this amount seemed to satisfy John. He made his way to a table in the back. I attempted to pay the bill with my debit card and found out that I couldn't buy gas for my truck and lunch for John on the same day without hitting the daily limit on my debit card.

By the time I joined John, he was in full consumer mode. Silently as always, John ate his lunch with only an occasional grunt or sigh, enjoying each bite. I ate my meal, trying to ignore the glances of the other diners. I wondered why John wanted cocktail sauce and tartar sauce, and now I knew. He used the cocktail sauce for his shrimp and the tartar sauce for his fries. I thought it was a little strange, but it is John after all. Finally, there was nothing left except a mountain of shrimp tails and empty plates.

As John was attempting to clean a combination cocktail and tartar sauce stains off the front of his shirt, I asked him what the big thing he had to tell me was. I told him it had better equal the value of all the food he ordered that had just maxed out my debit card.

"Brother Chris, you may not be able to tell, but I am very angry and upset. I saw this thing last week I got in the mail from a Grand Jurisdiction somewhere up north. It talked about updating the way we deal with candidates and adapting to the changes in our society today. I agree with having a more hands-on approach to our new Brethren. Teaching them and guiding them through their first year in more than just the questions and answers is something that we should have been doing for a long time, but there was a part of the report that I have a huge problem with. It also talked about *updating the penalties* of the degrees. It stated that the required degree 'Oaths deal with *ancient* penalties which are obsolete, unbelievable, unacceptable and simply not relevant in today's society.' The publication claimed that '*thinking*' candidates are having trouble giving honest assent to our current penalties. And the 'oaths taken on the Bible are not *symbolic*.'

I have a real problem with that kind of talk. What would this Northern Jurisdiction like the penalties to be? I can just see a candidate kneeling at the altar and hearing '*under penalty of a severe wedgie, followed by a head noogie, and finally a wet willie in both ears, so help me God.*' Give me a break! *This is ridiculous!* Hasn't anyone figured out that if you change the penalties, you have to change the signs?"

John scowled at me as I giggled at the mental picture of the signs that would correspond to a wedgie, noogie, and wet willie.

"As I said, you would have to change the signs, and when you do, you are messing with some of the basic foundations of Masonry. I cannot believe that anyone would try to change those things."

John stopped suddenly. He glanced around as he took a deep breath, "With all due respect to all my Brothers everywhere, there is a lot we need to get better at, and there are things that we might need to upgrade, and yes, even change a few things. *The penalties of violating our obligations are damn sure not one of them!*

No one ever said that our oaths taken upon the divine scriptures are symbolic. They are absolutely intended to be taken literally. They impress upon our minds without any uncertainty at all that our obligations are never to be violated. They are life-changing, and they are life making. To change the penalties would be to change the seriousness of a Brother's commitment to them. I hate to be sarcastic, but *'thinking candidates'* can figure out just as all of us *'unthinking Brothers'* can; those ancient penalties were instituted in a time and a culture that made them perfectly acceptable as punishment for violating an oath to God. It sure don't take a smarty pants rocket scientist to figure that out. Yes, there are a lot of things we need to get better at, but our ancient landmarks and tenets should be set in stone and never, never, be changed."

John's voice got a little softer, "Sadly, Brother Chris, I think this *'changing the penalties'* thing all have a lot to do with ignorance."

"Ignorance?"

"Yup, ignorance, I don't think these Brothers who propose something like this understand what Masonry is truly about. They haven't traveled past the outer veil of our mystic order to seek the real beauty and understand those profound lessons and truths that lie beneath the obvious. And no, I am not saying that they need to read more. It's all right there in front of them, as it is for all of us. They choose not to look. There are Masons who have Masonry in their minds only, and there are Masons who have Masonry in their hearts only. But to truly live and understand Masonry to its fullest, a Brother must have it in his mind and heart. Only then will he be able to walk those special paths and receive that light granted only to those who truly seek it."

John's face was red, and he was almost pleading in the tone of his voice. "Brother Chris, having an *'orderly rewrite'* of our penalties is like rewriting the Holy Scriptures to make them fit some idea of our choosing. Or rewriting our U.S. Constitution because it doesn't fit someone's idea of our here and now. These writings and documents are timeless, and tampering with them in any way will destroy them completely, as will this idea of changing our penalties will destroy Masonry. These Brothers need to pull their heads out and see what they are doing. After they change the penalties, then what? Do we change the ritualistic degrees to make them more modern? They are just silly anyway, aren't they? And where will it stop? I promise you it won't."

Well, I finally calmed him down, and John was pretty quiet on the way back to the shop. When I shook his hand, I told him I believed he was right on with his assessment of changing the penalties. Still, the threat of a wedgie, noogie, and a wet willie would probably make me do anything. John threw back his head and laughed as he threw Ol' Blackie in gear and roared away.

PIZZA PICNIC AND THE PROPER JOURNEY TO THE EAST

Getting to know Brother John over the years, I have learned always to expect the unexpected. Unexpected is what I got last month. John called and said he was about half an hour from the shop and wanted to talk. That was a good start since I write this column every month about those pearls of wisdom conceived in his medulla oblongata and emanating (sometimes rather rapidly) from his oral cavity. The fact that the first word out of his mouth was talking instead of eating was a concern, but I was so busy that I didn't have time to dwell on it.

It was still a wild and crazy scene when John walked in. He saw me on the phone with a customer and just gave me a wave and attempted to wedge his oversized frame into one of the medium-duty but comfortable chairs in our waiting room. I caught myself stifling a giggle as I thought that John should have one of those *wide load* signs on the front and rear bumpers of Old Blackie.

Now for all you newbies, Old Blackie is Brother John's big black F-350 pickup truck, which he talks to regularly and has genuine feelings for. I really shouldn't be thinking about my Brother that way, but as I was taking care of customers, I watched him out of the corner of my eye, and he didn't look like he usually does. He didn't exactly look like he was sick or anything, just not in a good mood. I sure hoped there wasn't anything wrong. I finally worked through all the customers and gave Roger the see you later sign. He had seen John come in, so he knew that he and I would be going to eat.

"Hey Brother John, I am ready if you are. Where do you want to go?" I swear that he stood up and the chair stood up with him. For a good thirty seconds or so, he looked like he was trying to extricate himself from a very tight girdle or, for all you younger Brothers, a figure forming undergarment. Laughing at him, I reached to try to pry one of the handles over one of his hips as he took a swipe at me and said he would do it himself. I told him we could get the *jaws of life* out and get him freed that way, which made him throw me a look that cannot be adequately described in this upstanding publication. Let's just leave it as what he had to say wasn't very nice. I thought for a minute that we would have to let him keep the chair when it finally popped right off of his pooching out posterior and landed with a clatter on the floor.

As he headed out the door with me right behind him, I heard him growling about us buying miniature furniture for the waiting room. Once outside, I asked him what he was hungry for. Instead of answering my question, John pointed down behind the shop, where there are about three acres or so of tall oak trees and a couple of picnic tables under the shade.

"We can eat later. It looks like a good place to talk down there." John took off for the trees. He sat down under a huge shady oak tree, and I slid in on the bench opposite him.

"Brother John, are you ok? I know that there is a first time for everything but I have never seen you want to talk before eating."

He smiled a tired smile, "It's no big deal, Brother Chris. I get real depressed this time of year watching some of the new Brothers moving up the line and becoming Masters of their Lodges. Sometimes I think I have an unrealistic view of how everything is supposed to work. I get out and try to visit all the Lodges I can. I really enjoy it, and getting to see all my

Brothers I have known for a long time is great. I get to meet the new officers and watch them progress, or not, as they work their way to the East. But it's kinda sad watching some of these Brothers breaking their necks trying to skip chair after chair to get there and at the same time not taking the time to learn the stuff they need to know. It just riles the heck out of me. In this day and age of instant gratification, it seems like everyone wants to get to the top as fast as possible, no matter what. Most of those who take the shortcuts at any cost to get there realize sooner or later that they would have been better off if they had just been patient and had a better year. The ones that don't come to that realization probably should never have been allowed to be the Worshipful Master in the first place. But that is just my opinion. You know, leading with knowledge is a lot better than occupying a position in ignorance. Way too many of our Lodges and Lodge Brothers are having to deal with crappy leadership every year. It's no wonder we can't get Brothers to come to Lodge. In many Lodges, there is usually a lot of talking about what will happen and then, in the end, a lot of talk about why it couldn't be done. We have a lot of talkers and not near enough doers."

Just then, I heard a noise and looked up to see Cody, a Brother from a nearby Lodge who is just a Master Mason. We have quite a few Brothers from that Lodge and my Lodge that come to the shop for their regular maintenance and repairs on their car, and we talk Masonry too. Cody is our sales rep for our main parts supplier. It was his regular day to come by. I immediately introduced Cody to John and invited him to sit and listen to the wisdom of Yoda....er, John Deacon.

Cody asked, "What the heck are you guys doing down here?"

"Just talking Masonry," and before John could continue, up walked Marlon, Messer, and Bill, all members of Cody's Lodge.

Bill said, "Hey Brother Chris, we came to drop off Marlon's car to get fixed, and Roger told us that you were doing some secret stuff down here. So, we had to come down to see."

I made all the introductions and asked them to sit and, after bringing them up to speed, nodded for John to continue.

"As I said before, Brothers are getting to the East in their Lodges long before they are ready to do the job properly. There is a reason why it takes or should take five to seven years to become Worshipful Master of a Masonic Lodge. Heck, in Solomon's days, it took seven years for an apprentice to become a Master. Can you imagine what kind of work that apprentice would do if he was allowed to be a Master Craftsman after three or four years? Take a look at some of our Lodges. You will get an idea of what I'm talking about. The Masters that are taking over many of our Lodges are untrained, unprepared, and generally unable to draw the designs upon the trestle board by which the craft can pursue their labors. In short, they cannot preside over the Lodge and their Brethren."

Bill raised his hand to talk, and John nodded his way, "I started as Senior Steward. It took me six years to make it to the East. I appreciated every one of those years of having the time to learn each station."

"I commend you, Brother Bill, for being patient," praised John. "You did it the right way. You are as ready as you can be. Just out of curiosity, did you go to one of those Wardens Retreats?"

"Yes, of course. I went to it two years in a row. I learned a great deal there, not only from the presenters but from the other Brothers attending."

"Yup," John replied. "I hear that those Wardens Retreats are darn good at getting a Brother all revved up and ready to take over the reins of his

Lodge. They didn't have those retreats when I was getting ready to be the Master of my Lodge, but I see these Brothers who have been to 'em, and they are full of all the programs and knowledge from the retreats. They definitely are rearing to go. I don't understand why every officer of every Lodge wouldn't be chomping at the bit to go."

I saw John look past me and smile for the first time, "Looks like we got us another Brother on the way." We all looked around, and there was Brother Bob from my Lodge making his way down the hill to where we sat. John and Bob had met at my Lodge a year or so ago and got along real good.

"Hello, Brothers," he called out as he pushed his way to a seat next to John. "It looks like we got enough Brothers to open any Lodge we want."

"That we do, Brother Bob," John replied as he introduced Bob all around.

"What are you doing down here all by yourselves, telling secrets?" Bob chuckled.

"Nah, we don't really know any secrets," John smiled, winking at Bob.

"I was just telling all the Brothers about Brothers becoming Master of their Lodges before they are ready. I have seen it plenty of times before where a Brother becomes the Master and spends the whole year telling everyone how great he is doing instead of showing them."

"You got that right, Brother John," chimed in Bob. "The Brothers know the value of Masonic membership, that's why they keep paying their dues year after year, but they also know what mediocrity and failure look like. A large majority of our Lodges are failing due to a lack of leadership and training of its officers. There is no excuse for not being properly prepared to become the Master of a Lodge. But I have seen Brothers skip chairs and still be darn good Masters, but they also worked extra hard putting in the time to learn all they needed to before they got to the East."

"I agree, Brother," John replied, nodding his head at Bob. "But those guys are few and far between. Any Brother who served his five to seven-year apprenticeship and learned his lessons on the way to the East is nearly always adequately trained and prepared. Additionally, he usually is energized and full of ideas of what to do and how to do it to lead his Lodge successfully. Now, if you put this in your newsletter, Brother Chris, you need to put in there that I am not saying that a Brother who doesn't serve seven years in the line before being Master won't be a good Worshipful Master, but there is a reason why it should take that long."

I finally found an opening and jumped in, "But it's not just that Brother's fault. The whole Lodge and each Master's responsibility is to ensure that each of his officers is well-versed and trained in their respective office duties. What has happened to too many of our Lodges is that they watch a Brother move up through the chairs, and they see that he is not learning what he needs to. Instead of fixing the problem or replacing the Brother, they spend several years complaining about him and then actually letting him become Master when they know he will fail himself and the Lodge. This is why Lodges struggle and sooner or later fail altogether."

All the Brothers were nodding in agreement, and before anyone could say another word, we heard a terrible sound that sounded like a wild animal trying to get out of a cage. *"What the heck was that!"* one of the Brothers exclaimed, looking around.

"I think it came from John," I said, noticing his face was a little red.

"Heck fellers," John muttered sheepishly. "That was my stomach growling. I am a little late having my lunch cause Brother Chris here wouldn't feed me."

Before I could fire back at him, Brother Bob said, "I got it covered. When I saw all of you Brothers down here, I figured at some point we would need food, so I ordered......here it comes now."

We turned around and could see a stack of pizza boxes and a couple of legs coming towards us. John looked like a dying man in the desert who had just found the oasis. He grabbed the top five pizzas off the stack, and a face appeared.

"I guess I've got the right place," the delivery guy said as he dropped the last five pizzas on the table. He made a second trip to his car and brought back drinks and plates. We all grabbed a plate except John. He used the whole pizza box as a plate. John was already on his second pizza, much to the amazement of all the Brothers except Bob and me.

Between slices of pepperoni, John exclaimed, "Brother Bob, you are my favorite Brother in the whole world. Did you pay for all these pizzas?" Seeing Bob nodding, John said, "when we are all done, I'll give you some money to help pay for all of this."

"*Wait a gol durn second here!* John, you never offered to pay for part of any meal I ever bought."

Much to my disappointment, Bob jumped in before John could answer, "This is on me. I enjoy talking with all of you."

Bob got thanks from everyone, and we all got a little quiet while we were eating, and it didn't take long for seven Brothers to finish off ten pizzas, especially when you consider that John ate almost three and a half by himself.

Suddenly I realized the time and had to push John to finish his talk because I had to go back to work. He looked a little annoyed that I had asked as he wiped a dab of tomato sauce off his chin.

"Brothers, go back to your Lodges and make them understand that we can't keep doing things the way we have always done them. If a Brother really has the right intentions to be the Master of his Lodge, he will have no problem taking the time to learn all the stuff he needs to before getting there. Brother Chris, you've got to tell all your readers somehow that it's all of our responsibility to make sure the right men are selected to be officers and that they get the right training to be ready. You have to make them understand that the griping about it has to stop, and things need to be done, *Now!*"

"Thanks, John," I said, getting up. "I have to get back to work. But you Brothers can stay as long as you want." I shook hands all around and headed back up the hill to the office. Just before I walked in the door, I looked back at my Brothers as they said their goodbyes. I smiled as I watched them shake hands and thought about that feeling you get, that Masonic feeling when a Brother returns that unique grip, you know he has traveled the same path, he has said the same words, and he has passed the same tests. It's a feeling that is almost impossible to describe in words but is felt by all Brothers, one to the other.

Thank you, God, for letting me be a Mason.

The Wardens Retreat and the Brown Noser

I was sitting at the Wardens Retreat's registration table put on by the Grand Lodge of Texas Education and Service Committee, checking in one of the Brothers for the weekend classes when the light above my table went dim. I looked up to see what the heck had happened, and I was staring into the face of the one and only Big John Deacon. He had a goofy grin on his face, and his giant frame was blocking my light.

"Whatcha doin, Brother Chris!" he boomed as I searched for his name on my list. "I heard that the Wardens Retreat was this weekend, and I remembered you were on this committee, so I figured I would mosey down here and see what all the hubbub is all about. They didn't have such a thing when I was a Warden."

As I scanned the list of attendees, "Uhh, John, I don't have your name on the list. When did you send in your registration form?"

"What do you mean registration form! I didn't know about havin' to register."

"John, everyone has to register so we know how many are coming and so we have enough food." That got him.

"Food, huh? Hey, can't you just add a good Brother to your list?" John gave me a little wink.

I sat there watching John raise and lower his eyebrows and winking at me with five Brothers in line behind him. I realized that this would get complicated, so I waved at Brother Tommy, our committee chairman. He is a Past Grand Master, and this was a job for someone at the top of the food chain.

After hearing my short explanation of the situation, Tommy gave me a confused look and led John away so I could register those who were supposed to be there. As they walked away, I called out to Tommy and let him know that if he allowed John to stay to charge him double for the meals. That earned me an over-the-shoulder glare from John. It was only about 20 minutes before I saw John walking across the room towards me, grinning from ear to ear.

"I'm in, Brother Chris!" John shouted, causing everyone to turn and stare. "Tommy says give me a name badge and a book."

"Sure thing John. Glad to have you. Which program are you going to take; Junior Warden or Senior Warden?"

"Are you kidding? I am taking the Senior Wardens Program."

"Do you realize that it is the program that I teach?"

John gave me a serious look and said with a straight face, "Brother Chris, I have been giving you a wealth of profound Masonic education for over four years, for free. Now I need some payback. I am here so you can give me some new and exciting Masonic education and it better be good because I had to pay for it. And thanks to you, I had to pay extra for the meals."

"Hey, I was just trying to protect our bottom line, just as I can see that you have been adding to yours. I can't help but notice the severely stressed buttons on your shirt."

John growled back, *"Cut the wisecracks!* I've told you a hundred times that you are not funny. Now tell me where I am supposed to go."

I had a couple of ideas in that respect, but I bit my tongue and calmly informed him what the schedule was and told him which room he was in. I was a little uneasy about having to teach him something. I have been writing down his words for a long time now, and I didn't know if I had anything that he didn't already know. But, what the heck, I just needed to do our program and hope I say something he hadn't heard before.

Well, shortly, the retreat got underway, with Brother Tommy thanking everyone for coming. We got the prayer and the pledges to the flags done first, and then he introduced the committee, followed by the Grand Lodge Officers. Finally, our Grand Master gave a short talk welcoming the attendees to the retreat. Every time our Grand Master, also a former member of the Education Committee, gives his talk at the beginning of the retreat, he says that during lodge visits, it is easy for him to tell the officers who have attended the retreats from those who have not. We are blessed to have had some great Grand Masters over the last few years, and it looks like the trend is going to continue for a few more.

It wasn't long before everyone had broken up into their respective groups, and the weekend was off and running. We got through the Protocol and Planning programs. Then we had a short group activity and discussion without too much problem. Since John didn't pre-register, he hadn't gotten the word that he needed to eat dinner before the Friday evening session because there would be no food at the retreat that night. Participants only had access to coffee and tea. Other than John complaining to the Brothers at his table and getting them all riled up, the only other distraction was during my planning lecture John's stomach kept growling, and boy was it loud. I asked Brother John to get a handle on it, but he just shrugged his shoulders. He did look a little funny as big as he is sitting at that little table with seven other Brothers.

We shut down the session a little after ten o'clock, and all I saw of him was his wide load heading out the door on his way to the Whataburger down the street. I went to bed a little stressed about this month's newsletter because it was obvious that John wasn't planning on sharing anything intelligent this month. I could only hope that something came out of the Saturday or Sunday sessions of the retreat. Something that is, that didn't involve John's belly or what he put in it. Good luck with that, right?

Everything got going right about 8 AM on Saturday, and I really thought that I hadn't given John any wow moments yet. Luckily, I had Brother Larry, who was on his *A-game* doing finance. Then Brother Clyde popped in and did his Grand Lodge Programs presentation, so I felt a little better. Heck, John didn't need to get his profound education from me.

Finally, we broke for lunch, and by the time I got to the dining area, the scuttlebutt was that John had gone back through the line three times. Hamburgers, potato salad, beans, and all the fixins covered three tables in the serving line. Usually, in their classes, the students at the retreat meet many other Brothers from all around the State of Texas. John, it seems, was accomplishing the same in the chow line. By the time I got through the line, most of the tables were full. I could see John had sat at the table with the Deputy Grand Master and talked while he was eating. Normally John won't say a word until he is finished eating. Eating, to John, is almost a spiritual experience requiring reflection without conversation, but he seemed to have broken that rule this time. I saw John return to the food line twice more while I was eating my lunch, and the last time the workers in the line just shook their heads as he scraped the bottom of the beans and potato salad pans. When I got back to the classroom to get ready for the afternoon session, John was already there.

"How's it going John, did you get enough to eat?"

"Yup, just barely. I got just enough to hold me over until supper, I think. Hey, I got to sit next to the Deputy Grand Master at lunch. He is a good guy to talk to. He sure talks funny, though."

Shaking my head at John's observation, "John, you talk exactly like he does."

"No, I don't!" John shot back.

Brother Larry was walking by at the same moment, "Yes, you do."

John stared at Larry and then at me. He finally got up and walked back to his seat, mumbling something about we didn't know what we were talking about.

We got started on the afternoon session right on time. The committee logged several miles of walking from class to class, giving their presentations. Brother Tommy caught me in the hallway between classes to tell me that he had ordered six more steaks with all the trimmings for dinner because of John. He added that we should have charged him quadruple for the meals. I agreed and ducked back into John's class just as Brother Jason was finishing up. All-in-all it went pretty well. The only hiccup was when I had to cut John off from his group presentation because he went on too long.

It had been a long day. Class after class, we taught our Junior and Senior Wardens as much as possible to prepare them for their journey to the East to become Master of their Lodges. This class was soaking up all we had to give and asking for more. The students and the committee were pretty much worn out and ready for the Saturday night dinner and traditional talk by our Deputy Grand Master. I had heard the talk twice already, and if John hadn't gotten his fill of Masonic education from the committee and me yet, he might get a wow moment tonight.

We all went to our rooms to get ready for dinner. Most of the Brothers brought their wives, so the couples usually dress up for dinner. Many of the individual Brothers, not so much. I figured that John would be in not so much group since Mrs. Deacon was not with him. Boy, was I surprised when I walked into the dining room, and there stood John (at the head of the serving line, of course) dressed in a suit and tie.

I walked over to him and gave him a low whistle, "Brother John, you clean up real good."

"What did you think that I had no class?" John asked indignantly. "That I was some hillbilly-redneck that would show up for a nice dinner in overalls or something?"

"No, I didn't think that at all. But I am pretty sure you wore that so you would not be confused with the servers and not be allowed to eat."

He got a big grin on his face and chuckled, "You know Brother Chris, you are smarter than you look. You got me dead to rights. I didn't want to take any chances."

"John, I am going to try to take that remark as a compliment and tell you also that you might as well sit down at a table because they aren't going to serve until everyone is here and we have the prayer."

"That's OK. I am just going to hold down the fort right here. I can offer my thanks to the *Big Guy* right here as good as I can sitting over there."

I shook my head, found a table, and sat down. Soon Larry and a couple of other Brothers sat down. Brother Tommy asked for the prayer. I glanced over, and sure enough, John was still standing at the head of the line. By the time Larry and I got in the line, I had lost track of John in the crowd, but reports were made up and down the line about how much food John had put on his plate. After I got my food and drink and made my way back to the table, I noticed that John had taken the last chair at our table and was nearing a clear plate.

As I sat down, John excused himself and made a second trip to the chow line. I asked the other Brothers at the table how much he had eaten so far. Their only response was *WOW* as they motioned with their hands to show how high his food was piled on his plate. Soon John was back, and though the conversation at our table was lively, John stayed silent until he had finished eating. When the last bite was gone, and he was satisfied that none of the rest of us had anything worth swiping off our plates, John sat back and let out a deep sigh, "That was some real good chow. Is there going to be any dessert?"

Before anyone could answer, Tommy introduced our Deputy Grand Master to give his talk. I heard it twice already at the first two retreats, so I sat back and watched some of the Brothers listening to it, including John. I could tell by John's expression that he liked what he was hearing. Also, he had stopped complaining about dessert. As soon as the talk was over, dessert was served. Somehow John ended up with two (what a surprise) and finished both before we finished ours. John then excused himself to go to the restroom.

As John was walking away, Larry said, "You told me how much John eats, but I don't think I got the total picture until today. Now I know what you mean when you say you have to take out a loan to buy him lunch. Whew!"

As we sat there relaxing before heading to our hotel rooms for the night, I glanced around the dining room and saw John sitting at the Grand Master's table with the Deputy Grand Master and the Grand Senior Warden. He seemed to be in deep conversation with them, but the Deputy was doing most of the talking. I saw and heard them all break out in laughter a couple of times, so I figured John was spreading his opinion on things, something he was good at. Larry and I remembered that we needed to go back to the classrooms to prepare for the morning balloting class. Once finished, Larry and I were on the way up to our hotel rooms and met John at the elevators. I asked John if he had a good talk with the Grand Lodge officers.

"They are all a good bunch of Brothers. I just stopped to tell the Deputy Grand Master that I liked his speech. He thanked me and said I was a brown-noser. Brother Chris, what the heck is a brown-noser anyway?"

While Larry was making choking noises in the background, I asked with as straight a face as I could, "You don't know what that is?"

"If I did, would I be asking you???"

"Well, John, it means you are a loyal Brother."

That brought a smile to John's face, "I thought so. He did seem thankful that I liked it."

The following day at breakfast, John seemed pretty chipper. After devouring a dozen doughnuts and a half-gallon of orange juice, he was ready for the morning program and graduation. I have to tell you that the Balloting program done by PGM Tommy is the most entertaining and enlightening of the whole weekend. At least that's what the Brothers who have been through the retreats tell us. I could tell that John learned some things he didn't know before. Soon we were handing out the diplomas for the graduation. It's pretty cool when the Brothers say how much they learned and how much they enjoyed the weekend retreat. I remember mine and how excited I was about all that I learned.

As John came through the line, he hugged everyone, and when he got to me, he whispered into my ear, "We need to talk after this. I have some stuff to talk to you about."

This gave me mixed feelings. It was good that I might have something to write about this month and not so good that John might have found out what brown-noser really means. Oh well, it was too late to worry about it now. John seemed pretty happy, so I was sure it was the former.

Later after we had cleaned up and packed up everything, I was checking out of the hotel when I got a call from Big John asking me to meet him in the coffee shop there in the hotel before I left. I found him way back in a back corner with a big iced tea in his hand and three dessert plates that had held some kind of pie.

As I sat down, John barely controlled his excitement, "Brother Chris, I had a lot of fun, and I learned a lot I never knew before. Heck, I am thinking about going through the line again just so I can do it right this time. You guys all did a heck of a good job with this retreat, and I am not the only one who thinks so. I also got to talk with Grand Master Jim, the

Grand Senior Warden Jerry, and the Grand Secretary himself, Tom. Those are some dang fine Brothers there."

"John, did you not learn anything about protocol this weekend? You don't ever call those Brothers by their first names."

John's face turned a light shade of red, "Yeah, I know, but those fellers treat you like you are their best friend, and it's hard to remember all that formal howdy doody stuff. But seriously, I got to have a good long conversation with the Deputy Grand Master, Walt, and boy, oh boy, is he excited. He has some great ideas and changes coming for us. Like our past few Grand Masters, he is out to make things better and is fired up. Do you know where Bedias, Texas is? Well, I do.... now."

"So what kinds of things did he tell you, John?"

"Well, if I told you that, it would be totally un–Masonic of me since he told me not to tell a soul. I will tell you, though; you need to hunker down and grab onto something because a high wind is coming through and blowing in change, good change. I think the last couple of years have started us on the road to be ready for the changes that are coming, and we are going to have a good ride, at least for the next couple of years."

"So, you are not telling me, huh?"

John had a big goofy grin, "Nope! You will just have to hang around and see what happens. I got a long drive ahead of me so I need to get going. As he got up, he stuck out his hand and gave me that grip.... yup, that one.

As I was standing there thinking how much I loved this old guy, John said, "Oh, and I found out what brown–noser really means .... we'll talk about it next month." And out the door, he went with a big grin on his face.

As I was mulling on that, the waitress handed me the bill for three pieces of pie and an iced tea. I turned back to the door just in time to see John pull out of the driveway. He must have known I was looking because he waved as he turned the corner.

"That big guy said you owed him," the waitress smiled as I handed her my card.

Yup, he's probably right.

Tiago's and a Chance to Spread the Light

It was a slow day at the shop, and we didn't have a lot of customers coming in. Roger and I were catching up on some backlogged paperwork and filing that we had been neglecting. The phone rang, and Roger answered it. He quickly put the call on hold and said he thought it was John, but he wasn't sure. I picked up the phone, and it was John. He was excited and asked if I could meet him for lunch. John said he had something exciting to tell me. I couldn't recall him ever asking me to lunch. John usually demanded that I go to lunch with him. Maybe he was turning over a new leaf and trying a politer approach? Ha, yeah, right.

John said he wanted to try something different, so I told him to meet me at Tiago's, a little restaurant next to the Bass Pro Shop just off of the freeway. Unbelievably I got there first. I grabbed us a booth along the back wall. I ordered a couple of iced teas and warned our server Randy about the doom that was getting ready to befall him. He just laughed (poor naive boy) and said it would be okay. I saw John come in the door. I could tell he was trying to be charming with the hostess girl. After a couple of minutes of watching an old man making a fool of himself, I waved and got his attention. John finally made his way back to where I was.

As John and I exchanged the friendly grip, "Hey, why did you interrupt me? She thought I was really funny."

"She was just being polite," I replied, rolling my eyes. "She just wants you to eat a lot. Like that's going to be a problem for you."

"Your usual sarcasm doesn't dampen my appetite. What is good here?"

"Well, I always get the sour crème chicken enchiladas. That sauce is different than any I have ever had, and it comes with the best borracho beans. As far as I am concerned, it is pretty close to the perfect meal." I waved Randy over and ordered my plate.

John asked for the same and then asked, "How many of them enchiladas can you get on a plate?"

Randy, not realizing what exactly John was asking, told him that the max was three.

When John told him to bring four plates to start with, Randy quickly glanced at me in disbelief.

"I told you so." He gave me a nervous smile and made his way towards the kitchen, shaking his head.

In about ten minutes, we had our food, and we got several curious glances from other tables as Randy and a helper sat down five plates, tortillas, and more chips and salsa.

John took a whiff of one of his plates, "This looks great!" Giving the John Deacon stamp of approval before lapsing into total silence while he ate. The only sound from that side of the table was an occasional mmmm. About halfway through all his plates, John motioned to Randy. When he came over to our table, John asked him if he could bring him six more enchiladas by themselves on one plate.

Randy asked, "Are you sure?" which got him an ugly stare from John.

"*Yes, sir! And sooner rather than later Pard*" he exclaimed.

Randy was back in a flash with the plate full and laughed, "The cook is upset because he has to make more of these cause we just ran out."

John just smiled and nodded and resumed eating. I sat there marveling at how much and how fast John could make food disappear. I wondered what was so exciting that he had to tell me. Then I was relieved when I realized that John hadn't caused any incidents other than making the cook mad. By the time John finished eating, Randy had cleared the debris away, and he was ready to talk.

"Brother Chris, you are not going to believe this, but I was sitting in the barbershop the other day, and the TV was on one of the news channels. A young man who I was sitting next to just out of the clear blue started talking. He told me that he was sick and tired of all the hate, violence, and crap going on in the world. He said there was no place where he could go to get a moment of peace to escape being slammed by all that was going on. I suggested that he go to church for a bit of peace, and he shook his head and chuckled. This young man told me that he wasn't sure he even believed in religion anymore.

Well, I was shocked, so I asked him why. He said that when he was young, his family always went to church. He said that too many times, he heard someone say that only those who believed what was being taught in that church would go to heaven, and this confused him. It made him wonder what was going to happen to everyone who didn't attend his church. As he got older, he saw all the bad feelings between religions. Each religion says bad things about another and the hate between some religions is hypocritical. He said that they all 'preach about love, tolerance, and goodness. Unless you belong to their group, they often practice just the opposite.' This young man said it's like you have to choose sides and decide to believe one way or the other instead of just believing in God.

I told him that he shouldn't blame God for all of that. He sat there quietly for a few seconds and finally said that he didn't blame God; he blamed religion. Before I could say anything else, he got called to the back by the barber.

I was left alone to my thoughts, and boy, did I have a bunch of them right then. While I sat there contemplating what he had said, I had to admit that I couldn't disagree with some of it. I think he expressed what a lot of people believe nowadays. Thinking about it, I had to admit that it was a little easier to understand why so many young people call themselves atheists. I suspect that many are not anti-God but just anti-religion. But for me, I couldn't stop thinking how lucky I was to have Masonry. Lucky for so many reasons.

I rejoiced in the fact that almost everything my young friend complained about is not an issue for Masons. For a Mason, the question of whether or not there is a God doesn't exist. Masons don't have to wonder. We know there is a God. He is known by different names to different Brothers, but he is real. He is a big part of our lives and our Fraternity. It's not surprising, I guess, that given the enormous number of different faiths, most, if not all, preaching a slightly different view of the same message, that people can become confused about what is and what is not correct. Of all the things in this world that are confusing, the existence of God and/or his message should not be one of them."

"I agree with you, Brother John. It is confusing for some people. We all know there are many hidden meanings in our Masonic lessons, and I believe there are many interpretations. Some are hidden in our laws and rules. Maybe there is more than one reason we aren't allowed to talk about religion in our Lodges."

John Looked at me thoughtfully for a few seconds, "That there is some pretty deep thinking on your part, and you might be onto something, but you need to pipe down while I finish my story.

Now where was I.... oh yeah, as I was sitting there by myself, I got to thinking about all that was going on in the world. I started beating myself up because I didn't tell that young man about Masonry. He didn't say he didn't believe in God. He surely had a relationship with the Big Guy at one time. If I had just taken the initiative and mentioned the Craft......

Then I got called back, and as luck (if you believe in luck) would have it, I ended up in the chair next to the frustrated young man. He gave me a nod as I sat down. I wanted to say something to him, but it just didn't seem like the right time or place. I sat there still chastising myself, but not so much for missing an opportunity to bring in a new member but more for not giving what seemed like a good man a chance to be a part of something that would show him the answer to all his frustrations.

Well, because I didn't have as much hair as he did, we got finished about the same time. I paid my bill first and walked outside. While I was fumbling for my keys, the young man came out, and I couldn't hold it in any longer. As he passed me, I told him that I was sorry for his frustrations. The young man shook his head and said he was sorry for bothering me with his thoughts. I told him that maybe he was supposed to bother me and that I knew of another place he could go to get all the frustrations off his mind. He looked confused, so I handed him one of those little card thingies' that have what Masonry is on one side and what we do on the other. I told him to read it when he had a quiet moment. He didn't even look at it before he put it in his pocket. I quickly assured him that I was not a salesman. The young man just smiled and said thank you. Then he was gone.

Brother Chris, for the next few days, I couldn't get him out of my mind. I knew he must have been pretty frustrated to say what he said to a total stranger. I just felt like I should have done more to help him."

"Hey, don't be so hard on yourself, Brother John. You did all you could at the time, and heck, you don't even know that you didn't help him."

John gave me a silent glare and growled, "I don't know why you keep interrupting me when I am telling you a story."

"I'm sorry, I was just......"

John cut me off and went right on with his story, "Well, there I was yesterday just driving down the road on my way to another sales call, and my phone rang. I didn't recognize the number but answered it anyway. The voice sounded a little familiar. The caller asked me if I was Mr. Deacon. I felt a little spunky, so I said that Mr. Deacon was my dad and that I was John. I don't know if he didn't get it or what, but there was a long silence. Finally, he asked if I was the guy who gave him a card outside the barbershop the other day. I was so shocked that I nearly ran off the road. I told him that I was the guy. He said that he had done some research on what he read on the card and had lots of questions. He said that he had asked his mother about Masons, and she told him to call his grandfather, who lived in another state. His grandfather is a Mason, and after talking with him, he was calling to talk to me about how he could become a Mason. I nearly drove off the road again. I was so excited."

I started to say something, but John gave me another glare, so I stayed quiet.

"The bottom line is that the young man from the barbershop is coming to the Lodge next week to meet the Brothers, and we will see what happens from there. What do you think about that?"

I just sat there quietly, and John finally threw up his hands, "Okay, it's time for you to talk."

"That's great, Brother; you did good."

"You know, Brother Chris, I can't help but think that the Great Architect himself put that young man and me at that place at that time so that I might have the opportunity to help him. I am so glad that I didn't screw it up."

John was so excited right then he yelled out (yes, he yelled out) for Randy. When Randy turned around, from across the room, John asked if he had any d-zert (dessert).... something choke-let (chocolate). Randy nodded and went to the kitchen. Shortly he arrived with two rather large portions of the best chocolate pudding cake with two scoops of ice cream on the side. I looked at mine and shook my head. Before I could say anything, half of it had disappeared onto John's plate. He quite rapidly consumed his huge dessert in silence, finishing well before me. John asked Randy where the facilities were.

John stood up, took two steps, turned around, and stood there in silence for a couple of seconds. When I looked up, he said with a smile, "Thanks for listening to all my ramblings. You know that I love you Brother; don't you?"

"And I love you too, my Brother," I said back, wondering what prompted that at that moment, and off he went to the restroom.

I sat there finishing my cake and ice cream, still wondering why he felt it necessary to say that right then. Just as I thought that John had been gone for a long time and that I needed to make sure he hadn't fallen in .... chuckle.... (as if that was even possible with his big anterior-posterior double-wide rear end).

Randy laid the bill down on the table, "Mr. Deacon said to tell you that he was late to a meeting and that he hoped that all of the very valuable material he was giving you to use in your newsletter was worth the price of lunch."

I was shocked... no... I guess I wasn't. I glanced at the bill as I handed Randy my card and whined, "*This isn't a lunch bill. It's a week's worth of groceries.*"

Oh well, I sure hoped it worked out with his new friend.

La Madeleine, Lemon Tarts, Mentoring, and New Brothers

"Brother Chris, What the heck is this world coming to?"

Working on an estimate for a customer, I didn't see Big John come in; Roger didn't warn me. I jumped at the sound of his voice. "Dang, John, you scared me! What are you talking about?"

John shook his head, "My mind is fried. I have been following a car for almost a hundred miles with its left turn signal blinking nonstop. I pulled up alongside the car to tell the driver, but he flashed me *you're number one sign*, so I quit trying to tell him."

"Why didn't you just pass him and forget about it?"

"*Quit trying to confuse the issue*! He should have turned it off. Let's go eat. I am starving."

I looked over at Roger, He was smiling and shaking his head. He motioned with his hands to get going, John was scaring the customers sitting in the lobby again.

As we piled into John's truck, "Ok, John, where do you want to go?"

"I don't know, let's just drive, and we will find a place. We will know where to eat when we get there."

We had been driving down the freeway for close to 10 minutes when John hollered, "*Pull over here!*" He guided me into the parking lot of an establishment called All-Stars, saying something about going to a sports bar. I tried to tell him that it was not a good idea and that it wasn't a sports bar, but he sometimes doesn't listen. He was hell-bent on eating there, so I pulled up right in front of the front door and told him to get us a table, and I would find a parking space. He disappeared in the door, and I just stayed where I was and waited. It took a couple of minutes longer than I thought it would, but finally, out the door, he came. He climbed into my truck without speaking. I got all the way onto the street before John finally broke his silence.

"Brother Chris, you need to wipe that goofy smirk off your face and enlighten me as to why you chose not to inform me that there were naked ladies walking around in there."

I couldn't help it. I had to laugh, and because I was laughing, John too started to laugh. "I tried to tell you, but you wouldn't listen," I started to choke. "What part of the words *Gentleman's Club* on the sign didn't you understand?"

"I didn't see that; I just saw the sports bar part," John whined. "You need to get me to some food quickly so I can get my mind straightened out."

"You pick someplace. But this time make sure you read the sign...completely."

John looked around, and La Madeleine Restaurant was coming up. "Let's go there."

"John, this might not be the best place for us to eat."

"Is there any naked ladies walking around in there too?"

"Uh, no, there is not but......."

"But nothing, pull in here. They are bound to have something I can eat."

I parked my truck. As we walked in, I explained to John that this was a French café and to keep an open mind. He ignored me as he went through the door.

Dear Reader,

I must tell you that when you first walk into a La Madeleine, you are greeted by a 10 ft refrigerated case full of French pastries and other delicacies. It's hard for any normal person, including me, to not be drawn toward it. For John, it was impossible.

John was staring at everything, oblivious to everything else around him. For me, I eat here with Pam every once in a while. She thinks I do it grudgingly for her. Still, I actually secretly like it because of a particular lemon tart; that is, in that refrigerated case. It seems to call my name every time I am in there. It looks like a miniature lemon pie about five inches in diameter with a graham cracker crust. I believe it is truly addictive.

Still in a trance, I called John's name several times before he acknowledged me and realized that several ladies behind us were waiting for us to go through the line. I let them all go first because I knew John might be a problem getting through the line. Finally, I coaxed him away from the sweets, grabbed him a tray, and got him in the line. He was checking everything out, and the confusion on his face showed he didn't know what everything was. That didn't seem to stop him, though, as he began to order several items. First, and to my surprise, he had them make him a chicken Caesar salad, which John complained didn't have enough chicken on it, so they kept adding it until he was satisfied. John then asked for three of the little fried potato patties (delicious) and two bowls of soup, one potato cream, and one French onion. I was hoping John was done because I knew he wasn't going to pay the bill. I ordered my usual French dip sandwich and a bowl of French onion soup. I paid and went to look for John. I found him at the bread display, getting some bread to go with his soup. If I hadn't reached in front of him for my bread, I wouldn't have gotten any at all because John cleaned it out. It wasn't hard finding the table John had chosen. It had enough food on it for four people. When only John and I sat down, it drew some stares from our closest neighbors. He fell into a deep silence as he ate. I took that time to enjoy my sandwich and think about the lemon tart I would get when I was done. Finally, John finished. Satisfied with his meal, he leaned back with a sigh and fixed on me with a steady stare. I waited until finally, John started talking.

"Brother Chris, I feel like I am always angry about something. This week I got a communication through e-mail. A Brother gave the membership numbers for our Fraternity. In 2002 there were 123,588 Masons, and in 2011 there were 88,896. He predicted that in 5 to 10 years, we will be down to 30,000 Masons. This Brother puts the blame squarely on the Grand Lodge officers for our predicament. Instead of taking all those pats on the back and all those photo ops, he said they should find a way to stem the loss. Every Brother is entitled to his own opinion. I respect every Brothers' opinion, so I am going to give mine on the membership matter only. I have been around for a while. I talk to a lot of Brothers, and I hear that this year less than 10% of the Lodges out there have even tried to put the new *Pass It On* program that the Grand Master and Grand Lodge introduced barely a year ago into effect. Brother Chris, you are a District Deputy; just out of curiosity, how many of the Lodges in your District have put or are trying to put that program into effect?"

Shaking my head, "I am sad to say, Brother John, that only two of my nine Lodges are doing it."

"Do you see what I am talking about!"

Several diners turned to look in our direction. John was getting all worked up, and I had to keep giving him the *talk softer* sign because he was getting louder as he talked. However, there was no stopping him as he rolled on.

"Here is a good program that has been proven in other Grand jurisdictions to increase and retain membership. This is a problem that all Texas Masons agree needs to be solved, and the Lodges are not using it. You know the reasons why they are not using it? Not enough time, we already do something similar, we are not interested, it won't work in our Lodge, the Brothers will never do it, ... etc., etc. It's the same old stuff. It's always someone else's fault, and usually, the Grand Lodge is the first in line.

You can go into any Lodge and find past programs offered by the Grand Lodge, gathering dust in the bottom of a drawer or thrown in a cabinet somewhere. There have been some really good programs offered by the Grand Lodge over the years, and a large majority of the Lodge's won't even try them. The Grand Lodge can't force any Lodge to use an offered program. It can only give each Lodge the tools to make their Lodge successful. My Daddy always said, 'you can lead a horse to water, but you can't make him drink.' Well, our horses just ain't drinking.

We have two big problems with our Lodges. First, we have poor leadership, and we elect the wrong men to lead us. We have too many unqualified and uninspired Worshipful Masters. They are uninterested and sometimes unable to effect any changes in their Lodge, leading to the second big problem.

We have Lodges that have stopped working. They have given up. Those men who would-be movers and shakers and who could reinvigorate their Lodge have given up fighting with those who oppose any kind of change. We all lose, every one of us. That's when the finger-pointing starts, 'it must be the Grand Lodges fault.' I think that most Masons are pretty darn smart, and you would think that they would be smart enough to figure out that the Grand Lodge can only be as strong as the Lodges are strong. Do you remember the old saying that feller Einstein said, 'the definition of insanity is continually doing the same thing the same way and expecting a different result?' Well, that is us for sure. How hypocritical is it to be handed a program by the Grand Lodge, which is proven to attract and retain membership, and refuse to use it? Then complain that the Grand Lodge needs to do more to solve the loss of membership problem. Hell, it gives me a headache just talking about it. My dad also used to say, 'some people would complain if they got hanged with a new rope.' That describes a lot of Masons.

This might have a familiar ring to it. Y'all need to stop asking what the Grand Lodge and your Lodge can do for you and start asking yourself what you can do for your Lodge and your Grand Lodge. Then and only then will things change and get better. We have way too few Brothers doing everything and way too many Brothers doing nothing and complaining about everything. We have had some dang fine Grand Lodge officers in the past, and it looks like we have some good ones coming up, but they can't do it alone. They can't force each Lodge to do the right thing. Blue Lodges need to take the blinders off, look at the big picture, and make decisions for the future of their Lodges and for the future of Masonry. If they want to know who is to blame for all their troubles, they only need to look in the mirror. Lodges need to stop wasting their time trying to lure, coerce, sweet talk, and trick Brothers into coming back to Lodge who haven't been there for years. I have a news flash, they are not coming back! Asking or begging them to come back won't get them back in the Lodge. If and when they come back, it will be the same way they came in the first place... '*of their own free will and accord.*' The way to keep them is to not let them leave in the first place. And I can't believe I have to actually say this, but that involves mentoring, education, and making them part of your Masonic family from the get-go. If you say, 'that ain't the way we always did it,' then I say, *that's why we are where we are now.*

Suppose you think that barring a Brother from a business meeting and an opportunity to learn how Masons conduct themselves gives him a greater incentive to get his work done faster. In that case, you don't have your hand on the pulse of our Fraternity. This ain't your Grand Daddy's Lodge anymore. It's not ever going to be again. There are good men out there who want Masonry and who need Masonry, but we are too pigheaded to go out and talk to them about it. They don't want the work shortened or to learn less. On the contrary, they want to learn more. They don't want the Ritual, or the work changed. If we talked to a Brother who walked away from Masonry, we would find out how bad we have messed up. But all is not lost, Brother Chris. We have opportunities to make it right and bring in these good men and to keep them. Those opportunities lie in mentoring programs like the *Pass It On* program. And I will say one more thing to all the Brothers, are you getting all of this Brother Chris?"

"Good God, John, I am writing as fast as I can," I gasped out of breath. "Can't you talk a little slower?"

John just glared at me and said in a much softer voice than before, "I want to say to all the Brothers, if you are going to Lodge, ask to work on a committee or find something to do for your Lodge. It doesn't have to be big; it just has to be something. Don't just sit there and take; give back. Every Brother has something good to offer his Lodge, so offer it. It's a whole lot more satisfying and fun. If you aren't going to Lodge, but you can, then go once in a while. Don't go once and decide not to go back. You didn't marry the love of your life after only one date; give it a chance. Make a difference. If your Lodge ain't floating your boat...wait a minute...why are you staring at me for Brother Chris? Don't you savvy float your boat? It's like tickling your fancy or, or.... never mind. I am trying to say that if your Lodge ain't making you happy, then find one that does. There are a lot of good ones out there. Don't just go home."

John abruptly stopped. The man sitting with his wife at the next table could hear everything John was saying. The man motioned towards John, "I don't know what organization you are talking about, but I have an idea, and what he said is correct. Good luck trying to change it, though. People have found out that it is easier to blame someone else instead of taking responsibility for something and just fixing it."

Then a man on the other side of us chimed in, "You are both right. What you are going through is bigger than you think. It's a miniature version of our country and our world. Until we change people's way of thinking, nothing will change."

Both men and their wives got up to leave and came over to shake our hands; one asked, "Just what organization is it that you belong to?"

"We are Freemasons," John said proudly.

"My dad was a Mason, and he never asked me if I wanted to be one. I just figured he didn't want me in there with him."

John cocked his head at me and gave me a *see what I mean* look. I quickly hauled out a couple of my *What is a Mason* cards along with my business card and gave each one. They thanked John and told him that they liked his talk and turned to shake my hand too, and then left.

When I turned back around, John was gone. I figured he went to the restroom since I had already paid for the meal. Then I saw him coming towards me with a tray. When he sat it down at the table, there were seven lemon tarts on it. He gave me an evil eye as I reached for one, but he didn't try to stop me. Instead, he grabbed one and, in three bites, had devoured it. There followed a series of oooh's and mmm's, and as John reached for another, an older lady appeared at our table. She stared at John until he noticed her.

When he looked up, she said, "Sir, you took every lemon tart they had up there. I don't think that is fair." She just stood there with her arms crossed, staring at him until he slowly reached down and picked up one of those tarts and handed it to her. Instead of leaving, she said, "My husband Earl wanted one too." Slowly and painfully (I could feel his pain), John handed her another. She thanked John, turned, and walked away without offering to pay for them.... (served John right). That left him with only three left. The way he was staring at them, I didn't dare try to take another.

On the drive back to the shop, John whined about what a traumatic day he had had between the guy with the blinker, the strip club experience, and the old lady snatching his lemon tarts. You'd have thought he was having a breakdown or something.

We parked back at the shop, and just when I was about to say something like "give me a break," John turned, shook my hand, and said, "At least I got to be with my Brother; that made it all good."

What could I do? As much of a pain in my rear end, John is… the guy is indeed good as gold. I just told him I loved him and watched him drive off in Ol' Blackie. It's always an adventure with Big John.

SWEETIE PIE'S AND MAKING A BROTHER A BROTHER

Well, my term as District Deputy will end here pretty quickly. When it does, my travels around the state will slow down a bit. Last Friday, I was on the road to another Wardens Retreat. My Brother Larry and I left his house for a five-hour drive, when Brother John called to tell me that he would see me next week. I told John where we were headed. He informed me that we were going to be driving right by where he lives. John talked us into stopping for lunch. Larry and I were hungry. After checking our financial status, we agreed to meet John at a little place called Sweetie Pie's Rib-Eyes.

Of course, by the time we got there, John took possession of one of the biggest tables in the back. As we walked up, John shook both our hands (oh yeah, with that grip) and told us that we were in the finest eating establishment in that part of the country. From the wonderful aromas hanging in the air, I believed him. Wow, everything smelled so good. As we sat down, from the looks of it, John had already consumed two baskets of something. The restaurant staff knew John pretty good cause he just raised his hand and a cute young lady named Stephanie appeared with a couple of iced teas for Larry and me.

Looking at the menu, I saw that they had all kinds of steaks, seafood, and plain old home-style food, like meatloaf, pot roast, and such. I noticed all sorts of veggies and potatoes for the side dishes on the menu. I quickly decided (at John's suggestion) to order the chicken fried steak, added some fried okra, and some cooked yellow squash which according to the menu was served au gratin style with onions and cheese. Larry followed suit with the chicken fried steak but settled on mashed potatoes and green beans for his sides. John, of course, got two chicken fried steaks, and I think one of every side they had on the menu. I heard John order squash, spinach, okra, green beans, black-eyed peas, mashed potatoes, cabbage, sweet carrots, and gravy; lots of gravy. If my Grandmother were there, she would have praised him for covering all the food groups several times over.

It wasn't very long before Stephanie returned with our food, and all I can say is *Ohhhh, Wow!* Everything was great. The chicken fried steak rated probably in my top five overall, and that squash was the best I have ever had. I pulled a John and lost all interest in the conversation and just enjoyed my lunch. I looked over at Larry, and he was doing the same. John was in ecstasy as well. Once Stephanie found a spot for everything John had ordered, he began to eat. I noticed he started by taking one bite of every single thing he had ordered. He chewed with his eyes closed and savored every taste. I have to say it was truly a meal to remember.

As usual, Larry and I both finished before John. I had the bright idea that we should be getting on the road since we had a long way to go. Well, that didn't sit real well with John as he made a face and mumbled something about holding my horses. Finally, he swallowed the last bite and informed both of us that leaving Sweetie Pies without dessert would show a lack of respect to the chef. I knew where this was going, and before either of us could say anything, John waved at Stephanie and told her we were ready for our dessert. I started to protest that I hadn't told her what I wanted, and he silenced me with a quick wave and informed me he had already ordered.

"Brother Chris, nobody, and I do mean nobody can resist what I ordered."

I saw Stephanie come out of the kitchen carrying four small plates of something, and when she got to our table.

I looked at John and smiled, "How did you know to order Pecan Pie?"

"Heck, I've been to a lot of places with you, Brother Chris, and I got your sorry rear-end figured out. I wasn't sure about Brother Larry, though. Since he is already on his third bite, I think it is safe to say he likes pecan pie too."

I glanced over, and sure enough, Larry had wasted no time downing his pie. Larry probably knew what happened to food left unattended around John. The pie was no less fantastic than the meal. I was sure I was going to need a nap during our drive.

I glanced at Larry as I said to John, "We are kind of in a hurry to get going, but if you have some semi-intelligent words of wisdom that are legal to put in print for next month, I would like to hear it as long as you are quick about it. I know last month you were pretty riled up."

John got a reflective smile on his face, looked at Larry, then me, and then with a chuckled, "My Brothers, as Masons, we get to witness profound moments in some of our Brothers' lives every once in a while. I saw something last week that makes me smile every time I think about it. Our Worshipful Master got to do something very few Masons get the honor to do. He got to make his little brother a Brother Mason. Many pairs of family brothers are Masons, but rarely does an older brother get to confer the degrees of Masonry on his little brother."

I leaned in, "*Wow, John, I'll bet that was great!* Tell us about the degree."

Well, you would have thought that I stole a biscuit off John's plate by the withering stare he gave me. "I don't know why you keep doing that, Brother Chris, but if you could stop interrupting me, maybe I could tell you," he growled, turning to scowl at Larry, who thought it was funny that John was roughing me up. Once John felt we were duly chastised, the smile came back on his face, and he continued.

"Well, it was last Tuesday night, and the Brothers were all looking forward to doing this degree because it was the Worshipful Master's little brother. Everyone had practiced hard to be ready. You could feel that everyone was happy to be there. The Stewards had prepared a pretty good dinner. After eating, our Marshall and Master of Ceremonies took the candidate into the anteroom to read his reading and prepare him for the degree. The rest of us began to filter into the Lodge room and prepared to open the Lodge to start the degree. You could tell the Worshipful Master was a little nervous as he went through the ritualistic opening of the Lodge, stumbling a couple of times which was unusual since he hardly ever makes a mistake. As the different stations said their parts, it was apparent that he wasn't the only nervous one in the room.

We finally got the Lodge opened; then, we were ready to begin. The Worshipful Master took a really deep breath, brought the gavel down, and we were off and running. Once the jitterbugs were all out, the degree was going great with everyone doing their part perfectly. Then it was time for our new candidate to offer his devotions and take a solemn obligation to God. That is when everything went into slow motion for me. You know Brother Chris, a great man, once said, 'you can observe a lot just by watching."

"Hold on a minute." I interrupted John, knowing I was doing it at my peril. "That doesn't make any sense. Who was it that said that? I have read a lot of quotes from the great philosophers of our time, and I have never heard that."

Once again, John glared at me. The only difference this time is that Larry didn't laugh, which was good for him. While John glared, I just sat there looking back, waiting for him to explode. It was like Gary Cooper in *High Noon* waiting for someone to make their move. Finally, John broke the awkward stare down, "It was Yogi Berra."

I couldn't speak. I just looked at John, trying hard not to laugh. It seemed like five minutes before he said defensively, "Heck, it makes sense if you think about it. You have to step back sometimes and look at things around what is happening instead of looking at what everyone else is focusing on."

Sarcastically, I replied, "Okay, John, since it is the celebrated sage Yogi, I will give you a pass this time and hear the rest."

John ignored me and began in a low, almost reverent voice to tell the rest of his story to Larry. "As I said, everything felt like it went into slow motion for me. I could hear the familiar words of the obligation, but the emotion in the Master's voice commanded my attention. I heard his voice crack a couple of times as he spoke those words that would bind his little brother forever to God and the Fraternity. I listened as he spoke each word slowly and with obvious feeling as the enormity of the moment found its way into the lesson he imparted. I watched him take an anxious breath as the Worshipful Master showed his little brother the light he was seeking. I saw his fingers quiver slightly as he reached for his now Masonic Brother's hand to deliver yet another important lesson in Masonry. And I saw him look into his Brother's eyes and though not spoken, I could see the message pass between them... *I love you.*

I tell you, pardners, I wasn't the only one in that room with a lump in his throat. It was a moment I will always remember and a degree I will never forget. Brother Larry, and you too, Brother Chris, every degree we put on is special. Every one of them should be as special as this one was. Sometimes we forget how special each degree is supposed to be for that candidate. It takes something like this to realize that everything we do in a degree should be as perfect as possible. It takes something like this to remind every Mason just how important the degree is for that candidate. Brother Chris, do you know what it is that we are giving the candidate during the degree?"

Clearing the lump in my throat, "Yes, sir John, we are allowing them to be a Mason." Well, the look John shot me made me wish he had asked Larry the question instead of me.

"Yes, my Brother, we make Masons, but as another great Mason said to me once, 'It's deeper than that,' and it surely is. In that brief and special time receiving the lessons of a degree, we give that candidate the opportunity to experience something life-changing. He has the opportunity to come to the realization of the possibility of elevated consciousness of the mysteries and the morality and spirituality of the universe. Now I know that sounds pretty heavy, but it is a fact, and that is why we need to understand how unbelievably important it is to give every Brother as good and as perfect a degree as possible. We owe them all that. Even though some never come to that realization."

John stopped talking, grabbed his tea glass, and waved it at Stephanie, who came over and refilled all three.

"Wow, John, I sure wish I had been there for that degree. Everything you said is right on. We don't take it seriously enough. Thanks for a great story to tell the Brothers in the newsletter. Well, we need to hit the road. Where is the bill? I guess I have to pay for all these *profound* jewels of Masonic education."

Smiling John reached for the bill, "Not this time, I am a regular here. Stephanie has my credit card on file, so I don't have to look for it every time and won't be so shocked by the tab. You'd better get going before I change my mind."

John followed us out to the car. He shook hands with Larry and me. It occurred to me that John hadn't told us how the degree ended, so I asked him. John's grin reached from ear to ear.

"Well, I have never seen our Worshipful Master so proud and relieved at the same time. The Lodge Brethren were also happy and content. It was a special night for our Lodge, and it was a special night for Masonry. I couldn't help thinking as our new Brother was shaking everyone's hands in the Lodge; I *sure hope he is one of the ones who gets it.* I think he will be. Y'all have a safe trip."

Our five-hour trip went by pretty quick because Larry and I were pumped up about what John told us. We talked Masonry non-stop. We talked about a lot, but the conversation kept coming back to what John said and how important it is to give a new candidate that necessary first impression of the Craft. Hopeful that the candidate might be rewarded with the feeling that his life has changed for the better and that his new life, living according to Masonry's moral and spiritual principles, would undoubtedly make him a better man, husband, father, and citizen.

It was a great trip. The conversation was so intense that we made a wrong turn, and before we knew it, we were almost to Oklahoma. We had a good laugh and resolved not to tell Pam or Tami because they would never let us live it down.

The Adventures Continue in Volume III ....

A NOTE TO THE READER

Thank you for purchasing and reading my book! I hope that this book has inspired you and has become a valuable addition to your Masonic library. If you have enjoyed this book, please consider leaving an honest review on your favorite online bookstore website.

As a special thank you for reading this book, please head to www.perfectashlarpublishing.com to access free content and to stay up-to-date with our latest news.

Don't forget to pick up each copy of the John Deacon series:

The Profound Philosophical Pontifications of Big John Deacon, Freemason Extraordinaire

Volume I: March 2021

Volume II: April 2021

Volume III: May 2021

Volume IV: June 2021

ABOUT THE AUTHOR

Brother James Christie (Chris) Williams IV was born in Mesa, Arizona, on a working cow ranch. During his younger years, he and his family moved to Texas, back to Arizona, and then finally back to San Antonio, Texas, where he resides with his wife of 45 years. He is very devoted to his daughter, son, and grandchildren and loves spending time with them and his several nieces.

Brother Chris loves Freemasonry and is very devoted to the Craft. He is Past Master of Davy Crockett Lodge No. 1225 in San Antonio and a member of several other Lodges. He holds membership in the Scottish Rite Valley of San Antonio, the York Rite, and the Shrine.

As a member of the Grand Lodge of Texas Masonic Education and Service Committee, Brother Chris has, for the last ten years, assisted in the instruction of prospective officers in revitalizing, administering, and managing their Lodges. He has spoken at Lodges and Masonic gatherings all over Texas on various topics from History to Grand Lodge Law to our Degrees' philosophy and symbolism and much more. He has an enduring ve of Masonic Education and is committed to spreading Masonic light whenever and wherever possible.